Connecticut

Connecticut

Sylvia McNair

Children's Press®
A Division of Grolier Publishing
New York London Hong Kong Sydney
Danbury, Connecticut

Frontispiece: Stone house in Barkhamstead
Front cover: Goodspeed Opera House
Back cover: Covered bridge, Cornwall

Consultant: Dr. Bruce P. Stark, Connecticut State Library

Please note: All statistics are as up-to-date as possible at the time of publication.

Visit Children's Press on the Internet at http://publishing.grolier.com

Book production by Editorial Directions, Inc.

Library of Congress Cataloging-in-Publication Data

McNair, Sylvia.
    Connecticut / Sylvia McNair.
      144 p. 24 cm. — (America the beautiful. Second series)
    Includes bibliographical references and index.
    Summary : Introduces the geography, history, government,
economy, industry, culture, historical sites, and famous people
of this northeastern state.
    ISBN 0-516-20832-2
    1. Connecticut—Juvenile literature. [1. Connecticut.] I. Kent, Deborah. America the
beautiful. Connecticut. II. Series.
    F94.3.M38 1999
    974.6—dc21   98-19621
                                                         CIP
                                                          AC

Acknowledgments

The author is grateful for the assistance of many people in Connecticut, including Miller and Margaret Wachs, Ann and Tom Wilkinson, Barnett Laschever, Barbara Cieplak of the Connecticut Office of Tourism, and the personnel at the Connecticut Historical Society. Thanks also to Maddy Cohen, who doesn't live in Connecticut but knows the state well. These people supplied and helped me find great quantities of important and interesting material— far more than it was possible to include in this book. Four young Connecticut friends—Andrew, Benjamin, Margaret, and Sarah— have been an inspiration, and so was a visit to Turkey Hill School. And once again, thanks to Anna Idol, who has been a friend, colleague, and invaluable editor on many projects.

Robin

The Houstatonic River

Eli Whitney

Contents

P. T. Barnum

A Native American dancer

Lake Waramaug

Mark Twain

Dorothy Hamill

CHAPTER ONE

A Small but Mighty State

First it was a wilderness, a home and hunting ground for small groups of Native Americans. Then the Europeans came and cleared much of the land for small farms. They built boats to carry people and goods along the waterways and ships to take them out to sea. Small towns appeared and roads to connect them.

A village green was usually in the center of the town. But it wasn't the grassy, tree-shaded place of relaxation one sees today. It was a pasture, dusty and trampled by livestock. Still, it was the center of community activity, surrounded by colonial houses, taverns, and at least one white-steepled church.

Small towns soon became cities. As the twentieth century came to a close, cities and suburbs, crisscrossed by roads and highways, covered much of Connecticut. Railroad platforms along the neck-lace of cities in southwestern Connecticut were crowded every morning with commuters, many of them bound for New York City. Long lines of huge, noisy trucks filled the highways, carrying the state's industrial products to market. Yet two-thirds of Connecticut

Immigrants on their way to Connecticut

Opposite: Autumn in Woodbury

Geopolitical map of Connecticut

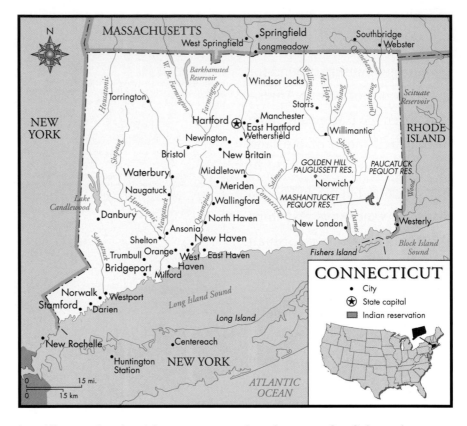

is still open land, with great recreational spaces for fishers, hunters, hikers and bikers, wildlife photographers, and bird-watchers.

Connecticut's beauty is soft and alluring, rather than spectacular. There are no towering mountains with year-round snowcaps. There are no huge canyons. Its beaches are not bordered by steep cliffs. Its waterfalls are modest, not gigantic.

But in Connecticut, one is never far from a rippling stream, a tree-lined pond, or a wooded hillside. Its longest border is a usually calm stretch of seawater—Long Island Sound. Its gentle, rolling hills are everywhere, covered with flowering shrubs and orchards in spring, brilliant color in fall, and puffy drifts of snow in winter.

Even in the crowded cities, parks and gardens are found every few blocks. Trees and flowers are planted along many highways. In midsummer, climbing roses tumble over the weathered walls of old estates.

Kent Falls State Park

Connecticut people think of themselves as being practical and hardworking. But they also take time to stop and smell the roses.

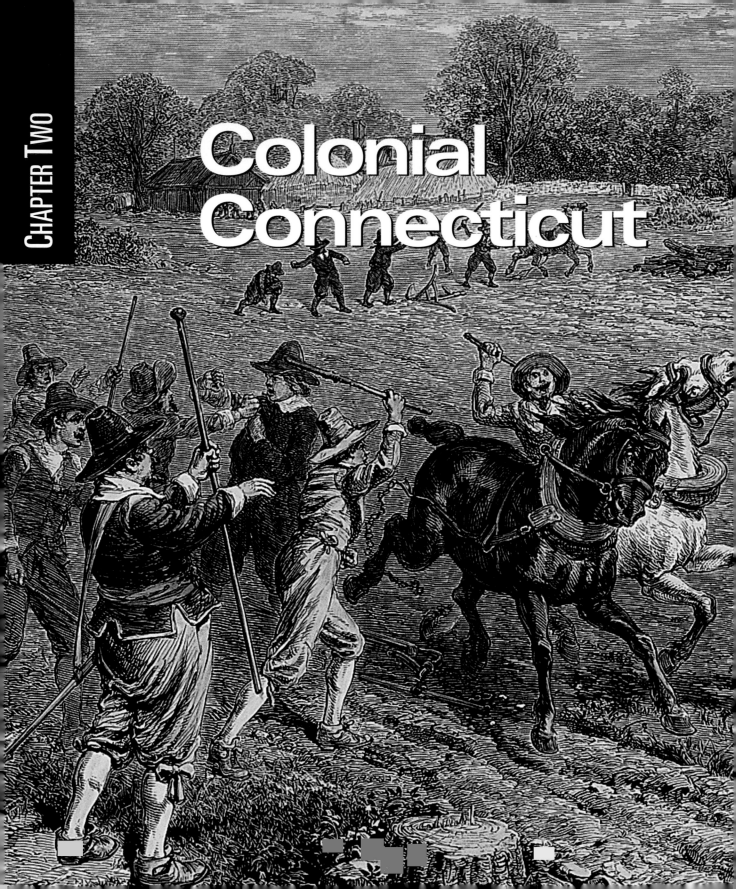

CHAPTER TWO

Colonial Connecticut

n the 1500s and 1600s, Europeans were excited about stories of the Americas. A few French, Dutch, and English explorers, fur traders, and fishermen were sailing along the coasts and up the rivers into present-day Canada and the eastern United States.

Kings and aristocrats saw an opportunity to seize new land for their empires. Adventurers were looking for places to make their fortune. Some church members, unhappy with the way their churches were run, wanted freedom to worship as they pleased. Other religious people believed it was their duty to convert all non-Christians, such as natives of other lands, to Christianity. These three powerful motivations—political power, monetary gain, and religion—brought a variety of people across the Atlantic Ocean.

In New England, religious motives brought the first settlers. A small group of English Separatists, the Pilgrims, arrived in 1620 and founded the Plymouth Colony. Other settlements soon

Missionaries meeting with Native Americans

Opposite: English and Dutch settlers in early Connecticut

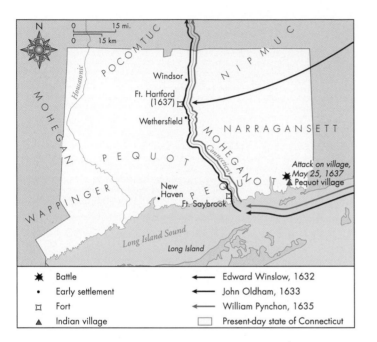

Exploration of Connecticut

followed. Puritans, people who wanted the freedom to worship in their own way, migrated to many places in Massachusetts and Connecticut. Several Native American tribes had used these lands for centuries for hunting, fishing, and farming. These "Indians," as the Europeans called them, sometimes fought over hunting rights, but they did not believe land belonged to individuals. It was just there, to be used by anyone who needed to hunt, fish, or plant crops. Europeans, on the other hand, believed they had a right to buy and own land, or simply to take it away from people they thought of as savages.

There were not as many Native Americans on these lands when the English arrived as there had been a few years previously. Thousands of them had died in epidemics of smallpox and other diseases brought by earlier Europeans. The Native Americans who were left were, for the most part, friendly to the new settlers, at least at first.

Connecticut Colonies

Early English colonists believed that the lands they settled actually belonged to their king. They had royal papers that gave them the right to certain areas. Robert Rich, Earl of Warwick, obtained such a paper in 1631. It gave him and eleven other English gentlemen rights to lands that included present-day Connecticut, part of Rhode Island, and all other land within lines extending westward as far as the Pacific Ocean! Of course no one at that time knew how far away the Pacific was. The sea-to-sea provision was repeated later in Connecticut's Charter of 1662.

Thomas Hooker is remembered as Connecticut's founder. A Puritan clergyman who left England for religious freedom, he came to the Massachusetts Bay Colony in 1633. He was not happy with the leadership in Massachusetts and felt Newtown, where he lived, was growing too fast. When he heard about a broad river and fertile valley to the west, Hooker set out with a

Thomas Hooker and his parishioners traveling to the Connecticut Valley

small group of his parishioners on a two-week trip to the Connecticut Valley. They took all their possessions with them, including their cows and pigs, and established a settlement on the Connecticut River. They named it Hartford. In 1636, Hartford and two other settlements, Wethersfield and Windsor, united to form the Connecticut Colony. A separate colony was founded in New Haven two years later.

The Fundamental Orders

Since the Connecticut settlers had broken away from Massachusetts, Hooker saw the need for a workable government. The Massachusetts Bay Colony was settled by Puritans, who believed they were the elect, divinely guided by God. Thus the government they set up was administered by church leaders. A government by officials who are regarded as divinely guided is called a theocracy.

Hooker was not exactly a democrat, but he believed that government decisions should not be made only by church leaders. He talked about his beliefs in a sermon that was later used by the colony's General Court as the basis for a document called the Fundamental Orders.

The Fundamental Orders said that government depends on the "free consent of the people." Voting privileges

Historical map of Connecticut

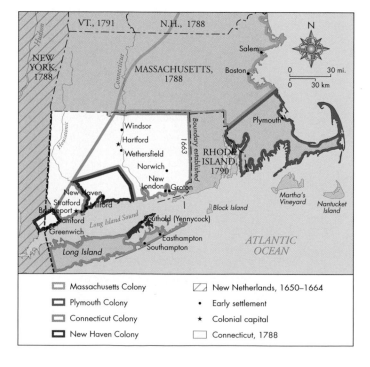

were given to white male property owners of good character, not only to church members. However, since the leaders of the colony all belonged to the (Puritan) Congregational Church, good character meant church membership to them. Thus Connecticut, like Massachusetts, was actually a theocracy.

However, the colony did not run its affairs from a central government. Each town, with the church at the center, made its own decisions. Townsmen elected officials to take care of day-to-day management. All eligible voters were expected to show up at town meetings and share in civic responsibilities. The Fundamental Orders also provided a framework for government, which was included in later official documents.

Thomas Hooker was a scholar; he had a library of more than a thousand books. He was tolerant of human weaknesses, but he believed the welfare of the majority was more important than individual liberty. Like most other leaders of his time, Hooker thought the best government would come from the leadership of a few competent, good men.

Relations between Native Americans and the colonists were mostly peaceful. But the Pequot Indians, who had emigrated from the Hudson Valley, resisted settlers' efforts to take away Indian lands in the Connecticut Valley. The Pequots tried to form an alliance with

Thomas Hooker

other tribes to drive the settlers out. In 1637, some ninety settlers attacked a Pequot village near the mouth of the Mystic River. They set fire to the homes and slaughtered more than 700 Pequots. Then they claimed the Pequot lands as their own. The following year, the English forced the Quinnipiacs, who lived near New Haven, to give up most of their lands and move to a small reservation.

The New Haven Colony

The Puritans who colonized New Haven had even more rigid ideas of right and wrong, if possible, than the leaders of the Massachusetts Bay Colony. They signed a covenant that they would be ruled by the "Word of God." Their laws were strict and the punishment for breaking any rules was brutal. The Puritans were especially harsh toward Quakers. One man was driven out of the colony, and when he tried to return he was whipped, branded on the hand, and banished again.

Many laws regulated individual behavior. They were called "blue laws." For instance, no one was allowed to leave home on Sunday except to go to church. Young women could be arrested for wearing clothes that were too tight; young men were punished for having long hair. People were fined for swearing and whipped for repeat offenses.

The Puritans of New England came to this continent to find a place where they would have freedom to worship as they saw fit. But once they were firmly in control, they saw no reason to share that freedom with anyone who did not agree with their beliefs.

In 1662, King Charles II of England gave the Connecticut Colony, including New Haven, a royal charter. This charter

King Charles II

included more guarantees of rights for the colonists than any other charter except Rhode Island's. Fifteen years later, however, King James II appointed a tyrannical governor, Sir Edmund Andros, and told him to revoke all charters and establish royal law in the New England colonies.

Colonial Life

Most of the Connecticut colonists were farmers. Soil in the river valleys was fertile, and soon the people were raising more than

The Charter Oak

Part of this story is history, part may be only legend. When the Dutch explorer Adriaen Block sailed up the Connecticut River in 1614, he spotted a giant tree. An English settler in what is now Hartford found the big white oak tree on his property, perhaps the same one noted by Block. As the colonist cleared the land around it, a delegation of Native Americans came to plead with him not to cut down the oak tree. They had held council meetings at this spot for generations. They believed that the Great Spirit sent them a sign through the tree each spring. When its leaves sprouted, the time was right for planting corn. The farmer spared the tree.

With the orders received from King James II, Governor Andros marched into Hartford with seventy soldiers. He demanded that the colonists surrender their charter. During loud arguments, the candles on the table were tipped over. In the darkness, someone stole the charter and hid the precious piece of paper in the trunk of the enormous tree. Over the years, the Charter Oak became a symbol of Connecticut's freedom.

Nearly two hundred years later, a huge gale blew down the historic tree. People came from all over the state to collect bits of the wood as souvenirs. A chair made from the wood of that famous tree is still used by the Connecticut speaker of the house. ■

enough food for themselves. They began to sell surplus crops and livestock to other colonies.

Farmers had to be self-sufficient in those days. Most of the work was difficult and backbreaking. The people had to clear their lands of trees and rocks—without any machinery. They built their own houses and made their own furniture, cut and hauled wood for their fires, made and repaired their own fences, carried all their water from streams or ponds, and planted and harvested their own crops. Neighbors helped one another, but in the early days there were no farm laborers to hire.

The colonists had brought pigs, chickens, and goats, as well as vegetable seeds, across the ocean with them. The Indians taught them about corn, a most useful and easy-to-raise crop, and how to grow beans and pumpkins in the shade of the cornstalks.

A farmer feeding his pigs in the early 1600s

Yankees

The name "Yankee" was a nickname used by Dutch sailors for the English settlers in New England. "Yankee Doodle" became a popular song during the French and Indian Wars. According to legend, British soldiers mocked the poorly dressed volunteers from Connecticut as "Yankee Doodle Dandies." American patriots from other colonies adopted the name and began to call themselves Yankees during the Revolutionary War (1775–1783). When the American Civil War broke out in 1861, Southerners applied the term to Northerners.

During World Wars I and II, people in other countries around the world began to call all Americans "Yankees." By vote of the legislature, "Yankee Doodle" is Connecticut's official state song. ■

New England Puritans valued education highly. They felt that everyone should be able to read the Bible. A few years after Connecticut was settled, a law was passed requiring towns to provide schools for children. In spite of the law, however, many areas had

Nathan Hale's Schoolhouse

Nathan Hale, a young school-teacher, is Connecticut's favorite hero. After graduating from Yale, he taught in a one-room school building that can be visited today, in East Haddam. He was one of the first teachers of young girls in the United States. He welcomed twenty females into the school for two hours of lessons each day. They came from five to seven in the morning, then left when boys arrived for a full day of classes.

Hale's career was a short one. He volunteered to be a spy for the Revolutionary forces and was soon captured. He was only twenty-one when the British General William Howe sentenced him to be hanged. Even though he never saw much action, Nathan Hale is a legendary hero of the revolution. He faced his executioners bravely and made a short speech that became a part of U.S. history: "I regret that I have but one life to lose for my country." ■

no schools in the early years. But as the colony grew, more and more schools appeared.

Reading, writing, arithmetic, and the Puritan catechism were the major subjects. Pupils were not expected to use their imaginations; instead, they were drilled to give the "right" answers to questions.

Yale College was founded in 1701 and moved to New Haven fifteen years later. This was the third college in the American colonies, after Harvard College in Massachusetts and the College of William and Mary in Virginia. Yale students (men only) studied

Yale College in 1764

Latin, Greek, mathematics, logic, and science. They attended prayer meetings twice on weekdays and spent most of their time on Sundays in church.

Yale College rapidly became the most important school in the colony. By the time of the American Revolution, there were nearly a thousand graduates of Yale. These men held many positions of power and influence in Connecticut. They ran the Congregational churches, held many of the public offices, and were a major influence in every aspect of colonial society.

Independence

Connecticut began to grow prosperous during the 1700s. It was largely self-governing, without much interference from Britain. Many of the civic leaders in the western part of the state had little quarrel with the Crown and were not interested in independence or revolution. But things were different in the eastern towns. People who lived there were not as well off as people in western counties. They wanted some of the political power held by men from Hartford, New Haven, and other western towns.

Meanwhile, the British Parliament passed several laws that threatened the freedoms the colonists had enjoyed. A number of consumer goods were taxed, including tea. In Boston, a group of men protested by seizing imports of tea and throwing them into the harbor. More harsh laws were passed in retaliation.

An organization called the Sons of Liberty, started in New York, attracted people who were determined to resist the British laws. Several hundred men in eastern Connecticut joined the society.

Jonathan Trumbull Sr., from the eastern town of Lebanon, governed the colony from 1769 to 1784. He was the only governor of the Thirteen Colonies who held office throughout the Revolutionary War.

A meeting of the Sons of Liberty

Colonists up and down the Atlantic Coast decided to send delegates to a congress in Philadelphia. These delegates were to decide how best to deal with the situation. All the colonies except Georgia took part in the meeting. Connecticut sent three men to the First Continental Congress in 1774. One of them was Roger Sherman. During his eight years in the Congress he served on more committees than any other delegate. He was one of only two men who signed the three most important documents adopted by the Congress. He helped write the Declaration of Independence and the Articles of Confederation, and signed both of them, as well as the Constitution of the United States.

The American Revolution

The Connecticut people were divided in their feelings about independence. A number of them, called Loyalists, were not eager to separate from Britain. Others, known as the Patriots, were determined to fight for freedom. But when British troops fired on colonists in Lexington and Concord, Massachusetts, on April 19, 1775, the die was cast. There was no turning away from the fight.

Eight long years after the first shots started the Revolution, the British signed a peace treaty recognizing the independence of the colonies—now the United States. England gave up its claims to U.S. lands between the Atlantic Ocean and the Mississippi River.

While the war was going on, the thirteen states had agreed to abide by a document called the Articles of Confederation. Each state would be independent, but they would give certain powers over to a Congress. There was no president or executive branch, and

Roger Sherman

A Hero at Bunker Hill

Israel Putnam was a farmer in northeastern Connecticut. Square-jawed and powerfully built, he became a hero during the French and Indian War. He was active in the Sons of Liberty, an organization that favored resistance to British taxation of the American colonies. A natural leader, Putnam helped convince Connecticut men to join the other colonists in their fight. About 3,600 of them set out for Cambridge.

Putnam won a place in history at the Battle of Bunker Hill. He was a brigadier general of the Connecticut militia, a group of men from Windham and New London counties. As the battle was about to begin, he mingled with his troops and advised them not to fire on the enemies too soon. His words have been quoted ever since: "Don't shoot until you see the whites of their eyes." ■

no federal courts. As time went on, it became obvious that the new nation needed a stronger federal government to solve its many problems. There were war debts to be paid. There were disputes over who owned the frontier lands west of the state borders. Federal laws were also needed to raise money for services that individual states could not provide.

To address these problems, a convention met in Philadelphia in 1787 to revise the Articles of Confederation. Fifty-five delegates chosen by the state legislatures arrived to accomplish that task. One of them was Connecticut's Roger Sherman.

Heroes at Fort Ticonderoga

Young Ethan Allen from Cornwall was a rough and colorful character. His early ambition had been the same as that of many other well-bred young Connecticut boys—to go to Yale and become a minister. But when his father died, he had to go to work to support his mother and seven younger brothers and sisters. He spent some time as a soldier during the French and Indian War, tried a couple of business ventures, then moved north to the New Hampshire Grants. This was the territory that is now the state of Vermont.

When the Revolution started, Allen was in charge of a group called the Green Mountain Boys. The small force, led by Allen and another man from Connecticut named Benedict Arnold, managed to capture the British Fort Ticonderoga (above). Later, during a skirmish with British forces in Canada, Allen was captured and sent to England as a prisoner. He would have been hanged, but he was such a popular American hero that the British decided to spare him. In 1778, he was exchanged for a British colonel who was being held by the Americans.

Allen's comrade, Benedict Arnold, fought in several battles and was greatly trusted by General George Washington. But before the Revolution ended, Arnold was persuaded by the British to spy for them. He has gone down in American history as a traitor. ■

The Constitutional Convention decided the central government of the young nation should consist of three branches—the executive, legislative, and judicial. Some of the delegates wanted membership in the Congress to be in proportion to the population of each state. This caused strong opposition from the small states. They were afraid they would be dominated by New York, Virginia, and the other larger states.

The Constitutional Convention, 1787

Connecticut Adopts the Constitution

Three Connecticut leaders helped to frame the U.S. Constitution. William Samuel Johnson (left) was a Yale graduate who served as president of Columbia College from 1787 to 1800. Roger Sherman was a self-educated lawyer and judge with a distinguished career in public service. He was a member of both the first and second Continental Congresses as well as mayor of New Haven. At the federal level, he represented Connecticut in both houses of Congress. Both these men were also signers of the Constitution. Oliver Ellsworth (right) was a Princeton graduate and a member of the Continental Congress and the Constitutional Congress. He helped Roger Sherman negotiate the Connecticut Compromise, but left before the document was signed. Back home, he wrote a series of articles in support of ratification. He later became one of Connecticut's first two U.S. senators.

Connecticut delegates ratified the Constitution on January 9, 1788, the fifth state to do so. The vote was 128 to 40. ■

Sherman is given credit for the Great Compromise, also known as the Connecticut Compromise. He suggested two houses of Congress, one based on the population of each state, the other with equal membership from all states. That's how Congress was set up—and still is today. The Senate is made up of two senators from each state. Only the House of Representatives is based on population.

Members of the Constitutional Convention ironed out most of their differences. They recommended that the finished document should be ratified by delegates meeting in individual state conventions. Delaware was the first state to vote for ratification, followed by Pennsylvania, New Jersey, and Georgia. Connecticut became number five on January 9, 1788.

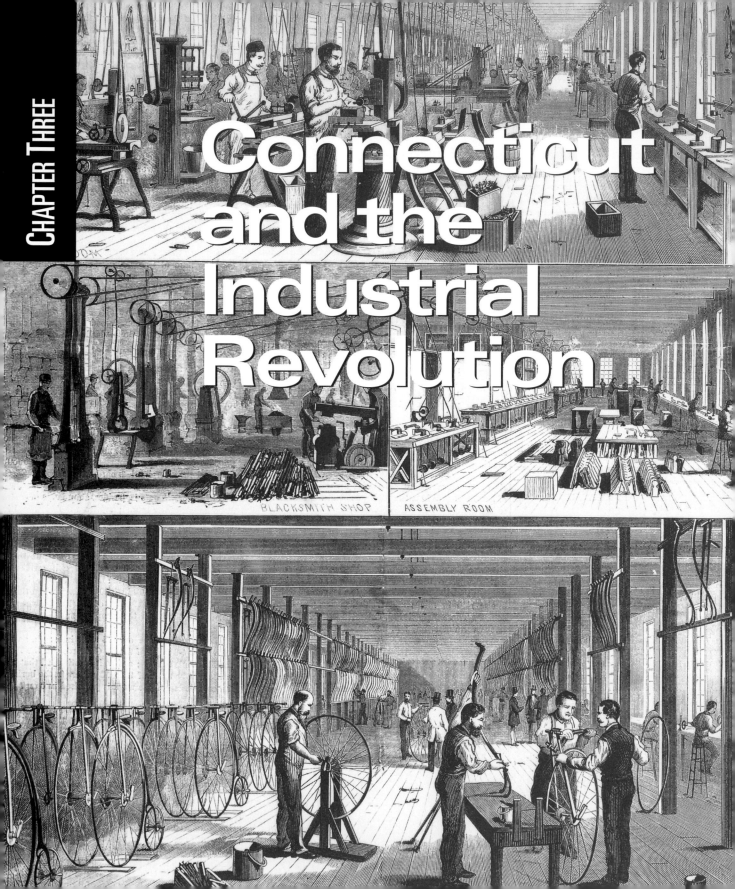

CHAPTER THREE

Connecticut and the Industrial Revolution

BLACKSMITH SHOP

ASSEMBLY ROOM

The first Connecticut settlers worked hard to clear their land and raise food. By the middle of the 1700s, some farmers had managed to become large landowners. They were now able to hire men who did not own land to work for them. This was the beginning of commercial agriculture. Surpluses of grain and other crops, beef cattle, hogs, sheep, and dairy products were sold. Merchants found markets for these surpluses in the British West Indies, Newfoundland, and even in some of the other colonies.

Connecticut at the beginning of the nineteenth century

During the Revolutionary War, Connecticut earned the nickname of the "Provisions State." Two men from the state—Joseph Trumbull, son of the governor, and Jeremiah Wadsworth—took charge of providing the American fighters with supplies. General Washington named Trumbull to the office of Commissary General of the Continental Army. In addition to food, the commissaries supplied tents, ammunition, soap, candles, and cooking and eating utensils. They also had to work out how to get the supplies to the forces. It was a huge task, and Connecticut played a significant role in the success of the Revolution.

Opposite: An early sewing machine factory

The Wolcott Family

Colonial Connecticut was governed by a very small group of aristocratic Puritans. This concentration of power in the hands of only a dozen or so families continued even after the Revolution. One of these families was the Wolcotts. They were as prominent in Connecticut as the Adams family, which produced two U.S. presidents, was in Massachusetts.

Three generations of Wolcotts served as governors of the colony, then the state. Ursula Wolcott was respectively the daughter, sister, and aunt of the three Wolcott governors. Besides that, she married Matthew Griswold, and both her husband and their son Roger were also elected governor!

The three Wolcott governors—Roger, Oliver, and Oliver Jr.—were wise, hardworking, and practical men. They were all farmers and also had careers as lawyers and judges. Oliver and Oliver Jr. were both educated at Yale.

Like most of their friends and colleagues, the Wolcotts were basically conservative, but they were living in a time of great change. As a member of the Continental Congress, Oliver strongly supported independence. He served as a major general during the Revolution and also contributed a great deal of money to the cause.

Oliver Jr. was secretary of the Treasury under President John Adams. After leaving this office and returning to Connecticut, he turned his attention to industry. He invested money in a woolen mill and helped a young inventor named Eli Whitney get a patent for his cotton gin.

Oliver Wolcott

Tapping Reeve Law School

Two buildings in Litchfield, Connecticut, are on the National Register of Historic Places. They are the mansion home of Judge Tapping Reeve (above) and a one-room clapboard building in the mansion's garden, where the judge taught aspiring lawyers. The Tapping Reeve Law School, established in 1784, is considered to be the first formal law school in the United States, possibly even in the entire English-speaking world. This is where U.S. law, as distinct from English common law, developed. Two vice presidents, three Supreme Court justices, a dozen governors, and 130 members of Congress were educated here. ■

Back in politics again, Oliver Wolcott Jr. served as governor of the state from 1817 to 1827. He helped draft the state's first constitution and worked for its adoption.

Connecticut Nicknames

Connecticut has had several popular nicknames since its early days. Each one illustrates a different side of its reputation. The name Constitution State comes from the theory that the Fundamental Orders, under which the colony was self-governing from its earliest days, was North America's first constitution. The nickname Provisions State honored Connecticut's role in supplying the Revolutionary armed forces. Some people have used the name Land of Steady Habits, because of the strong work ethic Connecticut people have promoted ever since Puritan days.

The Nutmeg State is the most colorful of the state's nicknames. It's not exactly complimentary, however. It refers to clever—actually shady—dealings supposedly practiced by early Connecticut peddlers.

Trade in many forms has been an important part of the state's economy from pre-Revolution days. Because the colony produced a surplus of agricultural and manufacturing products, men who had no land to farm made a living by selling goods door-to-door. They loaded up their wagons with clocks and tinware made in Connecticut. At Connecticut harbors, they bought spices and other hard-to-get merchandise from ships coming in from foreign shores. Then they set out with their wagons loaded to explore the countryside in search of customers.

Legend says they were sharp salesmen. To call someone a "Yankee trader" implied "let the buyer beware." And just where does the nutmeg fit in? Nutmegs were a popular spice in colonial kitchens. But sometimes a peddler would run out of nutmegs before finishing his route. So, according to legend, he simply carved bits of wood into the shape of nutmegs and sold them to his customers as the real thing.

The Rise of Manufacturing

Ever since its small beginnings in metalwork and clockmaking, Connecticut has been a leader in manufacturing. The 1800s saw an astounding number of patents for useful inventions issued to

A Yankee trader in the mid-1800s

Connecticut inventors. The cotton gin, a machine invented in 1792 by Eli Whitney of New Haven, had made possible the success of huge cotton plantations in the South. Samuel Colt, of Hartford, patented a pistol in 1835 that started a new arms industry in the United States.

Eli Whitney and his cotton gin

Throughout the century, dozens of Connecticut inventions led to new ways of doing all kinds of tasks. Charles Goodyear devised a method of producing rubber, a product everyone uses daily in many different forms. Charles Thurber invented the typewriter in 1843, and fifty years later G. C. Blickensderfer perfected a portable typewriter. Elias Howe patented a sewing machine in 1846. A coal-burning stove, an ice-making machine, a can opener, a pay telephone—these are just a few of many things we take for granted that originated with the creative genius of Connecticut inventors.

But the inventions were only the beginning. Factories sprang up in a score of cities in

Mystic Seaport

Mystic Seaport is one of Connecticut's most popular tourist attractions. A re-creation of a nineteenth-century waterfront village and shipyard, it is a busy place. There are shops and lofts where sails, rigging, and ropes were once made; a cooperage (for making wooden barrels and tubs); and a chandlery (for candles and soap). Visitors can watch people mending and restoring ships, fishers rowing a dory out to sea, and many other skilled artisans.

The village is on the shore of the Mystic River, near where it empties into Long Island Sound. There are dozens of historic buildings, including houses, stores, a school, a meeting-house, and a life-saving station. More than 200 rustic boats are moored in the river and harbor.

A sailing ship called the *Charles W. Morgan* is the last wooden whaling ship still afloat in the world. It is now a National Historic Landmark. Alongside it lie an 1882 training ship and a 1921 fishing schooner.

Young people enjoy the programs there. They learn how to climb the rigging on a schooner and study the basics of sailing, rowing, small-boat safety, and maritime history.

A museum in the village contains many ship models and artifacts of seagoing. During long weeks on board ship, seamen carved and etched pieces of whalebone into intricate shapes. The museum has a fine display of this unique art, called scrimshaw. Another popular exhibit is a colorful collection of ships' figureheads. ■

the central and western parts of the state to produce useful goods. Small manufacturing businesses had started in the late 1600s. Some of the first products were clocks and objects made of silver and tin. Ships were needed to carry Connecticut goods down the rivers and across the ocean, and shipbuilding soon became an important industry for the colony.

By the middle of the nineteenth century, trains were carrying salesmen and Connecticut goods all around the country. Carpets, soap, clocks, buttons, silverware, hats, locks and keys—the list of products manufactured in the state is impressive.

A ship being built by colonists

Slavery and Trouble between the States

Slavery was never widespread in Connecticut, and by the mid-1800s it had been totally abolished. Antislavery societies were active. Many people in Connecticut took part in the Underground Railroad. This was a secret network of people who helped slaves escape from their Southern masters and get to Canada. When Congress enacted the Fugitive Slave Act which said that escaped slaves in the North must be returned to their owners in the South, Connecticut declared that law null and void within its borders.

In the nineteenth century, most Connecticut people did not like slavery, for both moral and economic reasons. Although they were not ready to accept people of color as equals, they believed the institution

The Amistad Case

In 1839, a Spanish slave ship was discovered in Long Island Sound. The Africans on board had mutinied and taken over the ship, hoping to sail it back to Africa. Both the slaves and the Cubans who claimed to be their owners were taken into custody in Connecticut. The Spanish and Cuban governments sued in court for the return of their "property," including the Africans.

At the trial, Roger Sherman Baldwin pled the case for the Africans. He won in the Connecticut courts. An appeal went to the U.S. Supreme Court. Former president John Quincy Adams argued for the lower court decision, and it was upheld.

The *Amistad* case has not been forgotten in Connecticut. It was recently dramatized in a movie (above) directed by Steven Spielberg and is the subject of a beautiful sculptured memorial in New Haven. A replica of the ship, being constructed at Mystic Seaport, is expected to make a maiden voyage in the year 2000. The Amistad Foundation collection in Hartford's Wadsworth Atheneum consists of more than 6,000 objects relating to African-American history and culture. ■

PRUDENCE CRANDALL,
PRINCIPAL OF THE CANTERBURY, (CONN.) FEMALE
BOARDING SCHOOL.

RETURNS her most sincere thanks to those who have pat-
ronized her School, and would give information that on
the first Monday of April next, her School will be opened for
the reception of young Ladies and little Misses of color. The
branches taught are as follows:—Reading, Writing, Arithmetic,
English Grammar, Geography, History, Natural and Moral Philosophy, Chemistry, Astronomy, Drawing and Painting, Music
on the Piano, together with the French language.
☞The terms, including board, washing, and tuition, are
$25 per quarter, one half paid in advance.
☞Books and Stationary will be furnished on the most rea-
sonable terms.
For information respecting the School, reference may be
made to the following gentlemen, viz.—

ARTHUR TAPPAN, Esq.
Rev. PETER WILLIAMS,
Rev. THEODORE RAYMOND
Rev. THEODORE WRIGHT, } N. York City.
Rev. SAMUEL C. CORNISH,
Rev. GEORGE BOURNE,
Rev. Mr HAYBORN,
Mr JAMES FORTEN, } Philadelphia.
Mr JOSEPH CASSEY,
Rev. S. J. MAY,—Brooklyn, Ct.
Rev. Mr BEMAN,—Middletown, Ct.

Connecticut Freedom Trail

In 1995, the General Assembly authorized the development of the Connecticut Freedom Trail. Sites connected with the Underground Railroad and other aspects of the African-American heritage are identified as parts of the trail. The homes of Prudence Crandall and Harriet Beecher Stowe are identified, as well as those of two prominent African-Americans of the twentieth century—Marian Anderson and Paul Robeson. ■

of slavery was wrong. Also, they didn't want to see the open lands in the West turned into huge plantations with thousands of slaves.

Besides these feelings, most Nutmeggers—especially the Republicans—were intensely patriotic. So when the Southern states seceded from the Union and fired on Fort Sumter, Connecticut enthusiastically supported the Union. Within weeks, 50,000 Connecticut men were part of the Union Army. Connecticut factories produced arms, ammunition, clothing, and many other provisions that helped the Northern troops win the Civil War (1861–1865).

Education

The Congregational Church had been the leading force in all aspects of life in colonial Connecticut, including education. Early in the 1800s, responsibility for teaching children shifted from the church to the towns. Schools were small, with few materials. Teachers were overworked and underpaid. There might be as many as fifty children in one room, and their ages ranged from 4 to 17. In almost all cases, the only pupils were white boys.

Here and there, a few women started schools for girls. Sarah Pierce founded the state's first all-girls' school in 1792. Catherine Beecher established the Female Seminary in Hartford in 1824. Sarah Porter started a finishing school in Farmington in 1841, where household skills and moral development were emphasized. Prudence Crandall opened a school that included black girls, but local prejudice forced her to give up her mission.

One book written and published in Connecticut during these early years of statehood had—and still has—a profound influence on all U. S. education. Its author, who had taught in one of the state's one-room schools, was Noah Webster. His book was the first dictionary of the English language. Many editions have been issued since it first came out in 1828. More volumes of these dictionaries have been sold than any other book except

Noah Webster

A Family of Reformers

The Reverend Lyman Beecher, a Congregational minister, fathered an extraordinary family. He had thirteen children in all. Seven of his sons became ministers. One of his sons and three of his daughters became famous as leaders in the reform movements of the nineteenth century.

Catharine Beecher, the eldest, was born in 1800. She was educated in music, painting, and poetry, subjects taught to all "well-bred" young ladies of the day. She increased her own knowledge by studying Latin, mathematics, and philosophy. She believed that women

the Bible. Webster predicted that in another century American English would be spoken by more people than any other language on earth.

Two other Connecticut men helped to improve American education. Thomas Gallaudet founded the first school in the United States for deaf children and worked hard to raise both public and

should have the same broad education available to men. Catharine became a teacher. At the age of twenty-three she managed to raise money from various Hartford leaders to start a female academy.

Catharine Beecher helped found several schools and colleges for young women in other parts of the country. Later in life, she turned to writing. Ten of her books on various subjects of interest to women were published. One of them was the first book ever written on the subject of home economics. Although she wanted to help women live fulfilling lives, Catharine never became involved in the women's rights movement.

Her sister Isabella Beecher Hooker, on the other hand, was much more radical. She resented the fact that her father did not give her as good an education as her brothers had been given. She was also upset that married women had no property rights. Her husband supported her feelings and helped her persuade the state legislature to give equal property rights to both partners in a marriage.

Isabella joined with William Lloyd Garrison to form the New England Woman Suffrage Association, and later a similar Connecticut organization. She worked publicly for the cause with suffragists Lucretia Mott, Elizabeth Cady Stanton, and Susan B. Anthony.

Henry Ward Beecher was the best known of the Beecher brothers. In fact he became one of the most famous preachers of his day. A great orator, his sermons attracted thousands of listeners. He was a staunch supporter of the Union during the Civil War, as well as of the causes of temperance, abolition, and women's rights.

Harriet Beecher Stowe achieved wider and more lasting fame than any of her siblings. She wrote many novels, but the most important one was *Uncle Tom's Cabin.* It brilliantly and movingly exposed the horror of slave life on Southern plantations. It was also an amazing commercial success. The first printing of 10,000 copies sold out in one week. Within a year, 300,000 copies had been sold, and the book was translated into thirty-seven languages.

Uncle Tom's Cabin had such a wide impact that President Abraham Lincoln is said to have called her, jokingly, "the little lady who started the Civil War." Catharine and Harriet spent their later years at Nook Farm, in Hartford, near the home of Mark Twain. ■

private funds to support it. Henry Barnard campaigned for more state support and supervision of public schools. Believing that private schools created class divisions, he wanted public schools to be good enough to educate everyone. Barnard headed the first state school for teachers, in New Britain, which became a model for such schools throughout the country.

CHAPTER FOUR

The Twentieth Century

Connecticut was definitely a land of industry by the beginning of the twentieth century. Its factories were producing all kinds of products and they needed more workers. Immigration answered this need.

A flood of immigrants came to Connecticut in the late 1800s and early 1900s, mostly from Europe and Canada. In 1910, nearly a third of the people in the state were foreign-born. Farming was no longer very important to the state's economy. Nine out of every ten people in Connecticut lived in cities.

The Waterbury Button Company

Opposite: Forging guns at the Winchester Plant

DOOR THAT KNOCKS ON FULLER BRUSH MAN

A Modern Yankee Peddler

Albert C. Fuller (left) was born in Nova Scotia, Canada, next-to-the-youngest in a family of twelve children. His father expected all his children to start working hard at the age of ten. Al had almost no schooling and few talents. Yet in 1913, before he was 30 years old, he founded a company in Connecticut that was soon grossing millions of dollars a year. Its products were household cleaning brushes, and its salesmen, "Fuller Brush Men," became known to housewives everywhere.

Fuller started as a one-man company, making and selling his brushes alone. As he expanded the manufacturing, he hired men to go door-to-door selling the products. The company flourished for nearly fifty years, until lifestyle changes in the 1960s ended this kind of peddling. Albert Fuller is remembered as a man who treated everyone—employees, shareholders, and customers—honestly and ethically. ■

World War I (1914–1918) was a boom time for Connecticut. Several major weapons manufacturers were located in the state. Among them were Remington Arms of Bridgeport, Winchester Repeating Arms of New Haven, and Colt's Patent Firearms in Hartford. John Browning, who worked at Colt's, invented several new guns: an automatic pistol, a water-cooled machine gun, a light automatic rifle, and an aircraft gun. Munitions factories went into high gear to supply arms to Britain and France during the early years of the war. Defense production increased when the United States joined the Allies in the fighting. Eighty percent of the state's industry concentrated on producing goods for military use—hats, clothing, gas masks, and many other items.

The U.S. Coast Guard Academy had moved its bases from Maryland and Massachusetts to New London, Connecticut, in 1910. In 1917, the U.S. Navy opened a submarine base in Groton.

When the war ended, many factory workers were laid off. But business picked up again and times were fairly good during the 1920s. Then, in 1929, the stock market crashed.

Depression and Natural Disasters

The next ten years were bad ones in Connecticut, as the Great Depression spread across America. Business leaders found themselves penniless overnight. Banks closed. Factory wages were cut by nearly half—for workers who still had jobs. Millions of people around the country had no work. Only the huge recovery programs launched by President Franklin D. Roosevelt and supported by Connecticut's governors Wilbur Cross and Raymond Baldwin helped keep the state and country going.

The New London waterfront after the Great Hurricane of 1938

In 1936 and 1938, floods inundated many of the state's river towns, destroying lives and property. Before the flood damage was cleared away, more trouble came—the Great Hurricane of 1938. Without any warning, ferocious gales tore across Long Island and Long Island Sound, hitting the shores of southern New

Igor Sikorsky

Visionary men had been thinking about flying machines for centuries. In 1483, Leonardo da Vinci made sketches of a machine that looked something like a helicopter. In the years before World War II, several people tried to build a machine that could fly straight up and down and even hover in the air. A few experimental craft managed to stay in the air for a short time.

The man who constructed the first practical helicopter was a Russian immigrant living in Connecticut. His name was Igor Sikorsky. Educated in Saint Petersburg, Russia, he worked as chief engineer at the Russian-Baltic Car Works, where he constructed bombers used in World War I. After the Russian Revolution, he was broke and jobless. He came to Stratford, where other Russians were living, and made a living as a teacher. In 1923, with the help of friends, he founded the Sikorsky Aero Engineering Company.

The Sikorsky Company was successful in building planes for commercial airlines, and in 1929 it became a part of United Aircraft. Now Sikorsky was able to concentrate on the work that fascinated him most—inventing a workable helicopter. The first flight of his strange-looking contraption lifted off the ground on September 14, 1939. Only limited use was made of helicopters during World War II, but a new industry was started.

Igor Sikorsky was a warm, religious, and humble man. He was most proud of his helicopter's first achievement, in 1944, when it delivered blood plasma to victims of an explosion. He was always especially interested in the ways his "whirlybirds" could be used for rescue and humanitarian missions.

In Sikorsky's last days, he took great pleasure in keeping an up-to-date running tally on the total number of lives saved by the emergency-rescue capability of the helicopter. ■

England with dreadful force. Heavy winds continued north as far as the Canadian border. Hundreds of people died, many of them by drowning. Trees were pulled up by their roots, and houses were turned into kindling in moments.

Another Wartime Economy

War broke out again in Europe in September 1939. And, once again, Connecticut became the Provisions State. Factories expanded rapidly, and jobs were plentiful once more. Hundreds of young men boarded trains in northern New England as soon as they graduated from high school, and headed for Connecticut. Good jobs were waiting for them, to help build the engines, airplanes, submarines, ships, machine tools, and weapons needed for defense.

Air power was more important than ever. In Stratford, the Sikorsky division of United Aircraft produced its first helicopter. Factories lined streets and highways in much of urban Connecticut, especially in and around Bridgeport, the state's largest city. Many of them operated around the clock, with workers coming in on three shifts, six or seven days a week.

The nation was united behind World War II in a way it had never been before in wartime. For those at home, the war brought some advantages. Wages were good and people who had been living in poverty a short time before were now saving money. But there was heartbreak, too, of course. More than 200,000 men from Connecticut served in the armed forces, and many of them did not return.

After the War

Like the rest of the country, Connecticut settled into a period of peace and prosperity after the war. Families left the cities for the suburbs in large numbers. Gradually, some of the inner cities began to fall into decay, as many factories closed down or moved away. But Connecticut continued to be a leader in technological development. For example, the first nuclear-powered submarine, the *Nautilus,* was built and launched in Groton in 1954.

The first nuclear submarine, USS *Nautilus,* is now a museum in Groton.

In the field of government, Connecticut's constitution was long due for an overhaul. It had been in effect since 1818 and amended many times. In 1964, a federal court ruled that the state's system of electing state legislators was unconstitutional because cities were not fairly represented. A new constitution was adopted in 1965. For the first time in its history, the lower house in the state legislature would be elected on the basis of population instead of each city or town having one representative. Later amendments to the 1965 constitution set the voting age at 18 and banned discrimination on the basis of race, sex, religion, or national origin.

In 1974, Connecticut made news by electing a woman governor. Ella Grasso was the first woman in the United States elected to this office on her own, not as a successor to her husband.

Challenges Ahead

Connecticut has the highest average annual pay and the lowest poverty rate in America. Of course there are problems to be tackled, such as rebuilding decaying inner cities and reducing air and water pollution. But progress is being made.

The end of the 1990s saw the completion of a fifteen-year project to improve transportation. More than $11 billion was spent to improve highways and bridges, railroad lines, local public transit, and facilities at ports and airports.

Connecticut received a $7.8-million grant from the National Science Foundation in 1991 to develop new science, math, and technology programs in elementary and high schools. These are the areas where the greatest increases in jobs are expected. Students need to be taught problem-solving and reasoning skills.

Recognizing the importance of protecting the ecosystem of Long Island Sound, a comprehensive conservation plan was formed in 1995. Funds are being raised for cleanup efforts, through the cooperation of federal and state agencies, universities, businesses, and citizens' groups.

Testing for water pollution in Long Island Sound

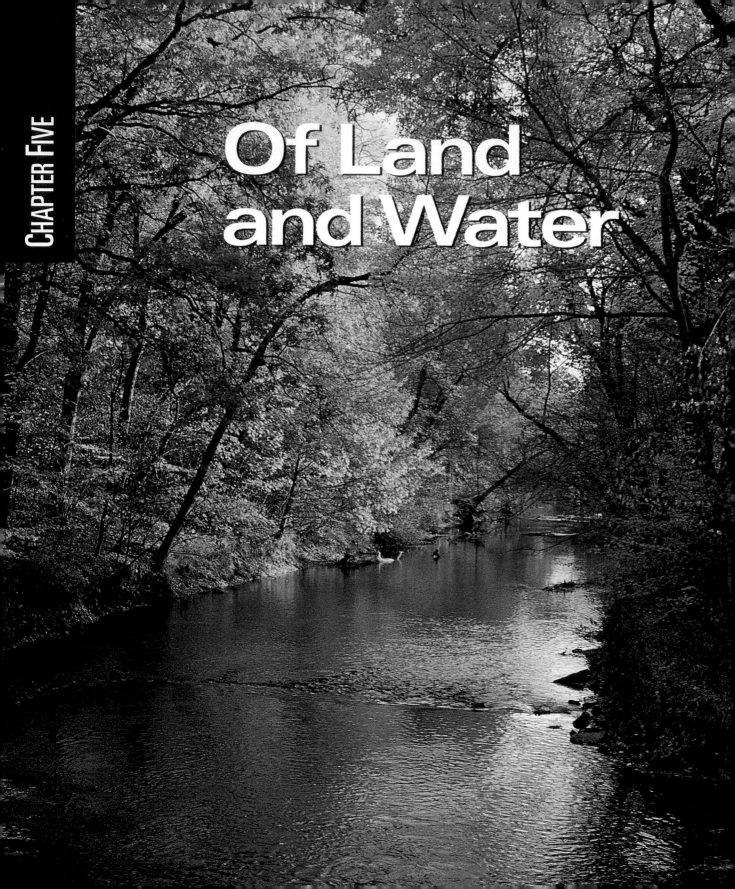

CHAPTER FIVE

Of Land and Water

onnecticut's southern border is a stretch of water. Sailboats float on the sparkling waters of Long Island Sound on every fine summer's day. And since no place in the state is more than 75 miles (120 km) from the sound, everyone can enjoy its beauty.

Connecticut lies in the southwestern sector of New England, with New York State on the western, Massachusetts on the northern, and Rhode Island on the eastern boundaries. Massachusetts also claims a tiny bit of the eastern border. Both Rhode Island and New York State also lie along the sound.

Connecticut is the third-smallest state in the nation, with 5,006 square miles (12,966 sq km) in land and inland water. Only Delaware and Rhode Island are smaller.

Autumn along the Connecticut River

Opposite: A rural stream in Milford

The Dark Day Legend

The first two weeks of May 1790 were unusually dark in Connecticut. On May 19, the daytime sky was as black as a moonless midnight. Birds fell silent; apparently they went to their nests to sleep. The legislators, sitting in session in Hartford, were convinced that the Day of Judgment had come. The lower house decided to adjourn, but a member of the Council (the upper house of the Assembly) did not approve of that.

Colonel Abraham Davenport scolded his fellow councilmen. He told them there was no point in adjourning, because if it were indeed the last day of the world, it wouldn't make any difference where they were. And if it turned out not to be the last day, they should take care of the important matters on the agenda. The other members were persuaded, and the Council went about its business by candlelight.

Colonel Davenport's sensible attitude became legendary. John Greenleaf Whittier, the most popular poet of his time, wrote some verses in his praise. The last words were "simple duty hath no place for fear."

What caused the darkness? No one knows for sure. Most historians blame a combination of distant forest fires and a solar eclipse. In any case, the sun came back to Connecticut. ■

Water has been very important to the history of Connecticut, as well as to the rest of New England. Much of the waterfront consists of bays, harbors, and beaches. Long Island, across the sound from most of Connecticut, protects the 253-mile (407-km) shoreline from most severe Atlantic storms. Three major rivers—the Housatonic, Connecticut, and Thames—feed into the sound.

Most of the early settlements were close to the sound or to a navigable river. The northeast had fewer settlers, as the land is hilly and rocky and not very attractive for farming. The Connecticut Valley, however, has deep, rich soil.

Landforms

Connecticut's land is rocky and hilly, with no high mountains. Its five main land regions are part of larger regions of New England

and New York State. The Taconics, in the northwestern corner, are the southern tip of the Berkshire Hills, a range of small mountains in western Massachusetts, eastern New York, and southwestern Vermont. The highest point in the state is on the southern slope of Mount Frissell, whose peak is in Massachusetts.

The Western New England Upland, between New York and the Connecticut Valley, covers about a third of the state. It slopes from northwest to southeast, with many streams and rivers flowing down from its hills and ridges. East of it is the Connecticut Valley Lowland, a strip averaging about 20 miles (32 km) wide, and east of that is the Eastern New England Upland. All three of these regions stretch north into Massachusetts.

The narrow strip of land along the sound is part of the Coastal Lowlands which extend along Rhode Island, Massachusetts, New Hampshire, and Maine.

Topographical map of Connecticut

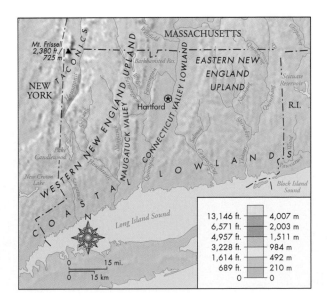

Living Creatures

Water abounds in Connecticut—rivers, streams, and waterfalls, as well as coastal estuaries and bays. There are more than 6,000 lakes and ponds. The two largest bodies of freshwater in the state are human-made—Lake Candlewood, in Danbury and several other towns, and Barkhamstead Reservoir, near New Hartford. The marshes and wetlands are home to large colonies of wading birds and a favorite stopover for migrating waterfowl. Ducks, partridges, ring-necked

Connecticut's Geographical Features

Total area; rank	5,544 sq. mi. (14,359 sq km); 48th
Land; rank	4,845 sq. mi. (12,549 sq km); 48th
Water; rank	699 sq. mi. (1,810 sq km); 36th
Inland water; rank	161 sq. mi. (417 sq km); 47th
Coastal water; rank	538 sq. mi. (1,393 sq km); 11th
Geographic center	Hartford, at East Berlin
Highest point	Mount Frissell's south slope, 2,380 feet (725 m) above sea level
Lowest point	Sea level at Long Island Sound shore
Largest city	Bridgeport
Population; rank	3,295,669 (1990 census); 27th
Record high temperature	105°F (41°C) at Waterbury on July 22, 1926
Record low temperature	–32°F (–36°C) at Falls Village on February 16, 1943
Average July temperature	71°F (22°C)
Average January temperature	26°F (–3°C)
Average annual precipitation	47 inches (119 cm)

pheasants, wild turkeys, and ruffed grouse are common, as are orioles, bluebirds, sparrows, thrushes, and warblers. Now and then a bird-watcher catches a glimpse of bald eagles, particularly near the Shepaug Dam, one of their nesting sites.

Forests cover nearly two-thirds of the state, giving shelter to white-tailed deer, foxes, coyotes, hares, minks, muskrats, otters, and rabbits. Black bears and bobcats are rare, but have been spotted occasionally. Shad, trout, and pickerel thrive in the streams. Clams, lobsters, and oysters, as well as striped bass, bluefish, and swordfish, are found in offshore waters.

Climate and Seasons

The state's woodlands, wetlands, farmlands, and coastal regions change their appearance in four distinct seasons. In spring, lacy dogwood and mountain laurel bring color to the woodlands and

Opposite: Lake Waramaug State Park in the Western New England Upland

The Housatonic Estuary

Estuaries are bodies of water where freshwater and saltwater mix. The estuary at the mouth of the Housatonic River consists of uplands (well-drained soils), tidal wetlands and mudflats, sand spits and barrier beaches, and Long Island Sound. These habitats support a great variety of plant and animal life.

All living beings are dependent on a food chain that begins with the plants and algae to be found in places like this. Tiny animals that can only be seen through a microscope feed on the plants and algae, along with shellfish, larger fish, insects, and four-legged animals. Bats, skunks, raccoons, and muskrats (above) eat the insects and small animals. Large fish and birds feed on smaller fish.

The Connecticut Audubon Society maintains a Coastal Center on a barrier beach at Milford Point. Visitors can observe the marshes from the Bird Sanctuary Boardwalk and an observation tower. Naturalists lead interpretive nature walks. Children come with their parents, teachers, and other adult leaders to learn about the importance of the Sound and the estuaries. ■

roadsides. Tiny wildflowers poke their heads through damp spring soil. Fields and gardens thrive during the summers. Extremely hot weather is rare in Connecticut, although its humidity makes for an uncomfortable summer.

In autumn, the woods are ablaze with the brilliant colors of fall foliage. A wonderful mixture of leafy trees covers the hillsides with

A mountain laurel in bloom

blankets of red, orange, yellow, and gold. Ash, beech, birch, elm, hemlock, maple, and oak trees provide the brilliance; pine and other evergreens balance the bouquets with shades of green. Tourists, locally called "leaf peepers," take to the highways and byways to enjoy the scenery. More than a hundred state parks and forests are especially popular with visitors at this time of year.

Then, before one expects it, winter blows in and suddenly the landscape is pure, sparkling white. Snow falls during the winter in every part of the state, sometimes as much as 80 inches (200 cm) a year in the highest parts. In lower areas, the average is from 25 inches (64 cm) along the coast to 35 inches (89 cm) farther inland.

Most of the state receives about the same amount of rainfall during the rest of the year. Occasionally the thermometers

Winter on the Housatonic River at Cornwall

The Flood of 1955

Townspeople in the Naugatuck Valley in western Connecticut woke up on August 19, 1955, to find floodwaters spilling over low-lying areas. Waterbury suffered some of the greatest damage in the loss of lives and property.

The Sikorsky helicopter plant in Stratford sent ten helicopters to help in rescue work. Three hundred National Guardsmen were brought in to prevent looting, help supply drinking water, and clean up debris. Within a week, more than 90,000 people had been inoculated for typhoid. Some of the wreckage from Waterbury was washed all the way down to Long Island Sound. Before the water receded, 164 bridges had been damaged or destroyed and 176 miles (283 km) of roads had to be rebuilt. Electricity was restored within a week, but it was nearly a month before gas was available and water was safe to drink. One military officer said the destruction caused by flood waters equaled the damage he had seen at the end of World War II in Germany. ■

record extreme temperatures—from a high of 105°F (41°C) to a low of –32°F (–36°C), but these spells of hot and cold weather don't usually last long. The state rarely experiences natural disasters. However, floods in 1936 and 1955 caused a lot of damage, and a catastrophic hurricane swept through the state in September 1938.

Natural Resources

The first settlers came to Connecticut expecting to farm the land. However, many of them soon found that the thin, rocky soil in many of the hills and valleys was not good for farming. The soil along the Connecticut River is rich and productive, but agriculture

Old New-Gate Prison

Mines are interesting places to visit. An old, unused mine in north-central Connecticut has a special fascination because of its spookiness and unusual history.

Early Connecticut colonists were searching for minerals and it looked as if they had found something valuable not far from Hartford—copper. This could be very useful. In 1707, America's first copper mine, the Old New-Gate, was chartered. The owners dug out a cavern about 16 square feet (1.5 sq m), plus some tunnels, one leading to a natural spring. But mining efforts met with little success, and after a while the mine was left idle.

In 1773, the colonial legislature was talking about the need for a gaol (that's how it was spelled then), a prison for murderers, burglars, counterfeiters, and horse thieves. Someone mentioned the old copper mine and it seemed a perfect answer to the problem. It wouldn't cost much to acquire it; few or no alterations would be needed. It would surely be secure—the only way out was by climbing the only shaft, which went straight up for 75 feet (23 m).

Ironically, the very first prisoner confined in this damp, cold, dark, rat-infested dungeon managed to climb out! Later, three other prisoners got away before the authorities built a high wall around the shaft opening. During the Revolution, the prison was used to incarcerate Tories—colonists loyal to the English crown—and British prisoners of war.

This horrible place continued to be used as a prison until 1827. Today, it is a National Historic Landmark, operated by the Connecticut Historical Commission. Visitors can descend a shaft down to the main room. Water drips down the walls of the shaft as guides make history real with stories about prison life in those days and about the escapes—some successful and some tragically unsuccessful. ■

Connecticut's rolling
farmland

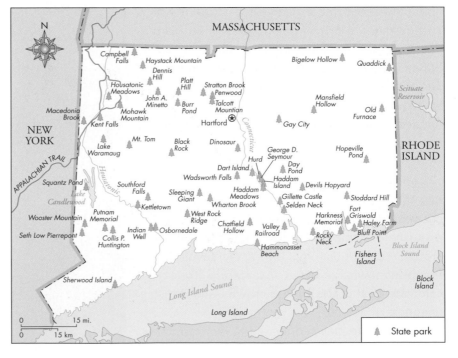

MASSACHUSETTS

Campbell Falls

Haystack Mountain

Bigelow Hollow

Quaddick

Scituate Reservoir

Dennis Hill

Platt Hill

Stratton Brook

Penwood

Mansfield Hollow

Housatonic Meadows

John A. Minetto

Talcott Mountain

Old Furnace

RHODE ISLAND

Macedonia Brook

Mohawk Mountain

Burr Pond

Hartford ⊛

Connecticut

Gay City

NEW YORK

Kent Falls

Mt. Tom

Black Rock

Dinosaur

Hopeville Pond

Lake Waramaug

George D. Seymour

APPALACHIAN TRAIL

Squantz Pond

Lake Candlewood

Hurd

Day Pond

Southford Falls

Dart Island

Wadsworth Falls

Haddam Island

Devils Hopyard

Stoddard Hill

Housatonic

Sleeping Giant

Haddam Meadows

Kettletown

Wharton Brook

Gillette Castle

Selden Neck

Fort Griswold

Wooster Mountain

Putnam Memorial

West Rock Ridge

Chatfield Hollow

Harkness Memorial

Haley Farm

Seth Low Pierrepont

Indian Well

Osbornedale

Valley Railroad

Rocky Neck

Bluff Point

Collis P. Huntington

Hammonasset Beach

Fishers Island

Block Island Sound

Block Island

Sherwood Island

Long Island Sound

Long Island

0 ___ 15 mi.
0 ___ 15 km

🌲 State park

Connecticut's **parks
and forests**

Wilbur Cross

Wilbur Cross was born and brought up on a farm in eastern Connecticut. Protestant and Anglo-Saxon, he became a professor of English literature at Yale. Connecticut folks with that kind of traditional background were almost all Republicans from the time of the Civil War until well into the twentieth century.

But the popular Professor Cross, nicknamed "Uncle Toby," surprised everyone by running for governor on the Democratic ticket in 1931 when he was seventy-one years old. Cross was elected, served eight years, and was responsible for pushing quite a few social reforms into law. He also impressed people with the leadership he showed in helping the state recover from the two natural disasters that occurred during his term in office—the Flood of 1936 and the Hurricane of 1938.

Connecticut honored Governor Cross by naming a part of Connecticut Highway 15 for him: the Wilbur Cross Parkway. ■

accounts for only 1 percent of the state's total production today. As a result, Connecticut developed into an industrial state. Its people used their famous Yankee ingenuity to become artisans and manufacturers, merchants and financiers. Sand and gravel are the state's only important minerals.

The state's woods, waters, and fields, which make up nearly two-thirds of its total area, are a very important resource for recreation. More than a hundred public parks and forests in Connecticut provide nearly limitless opportunities for hiking, fishing, canoeing, skiing, bird-watching, and many other outdoor activities.

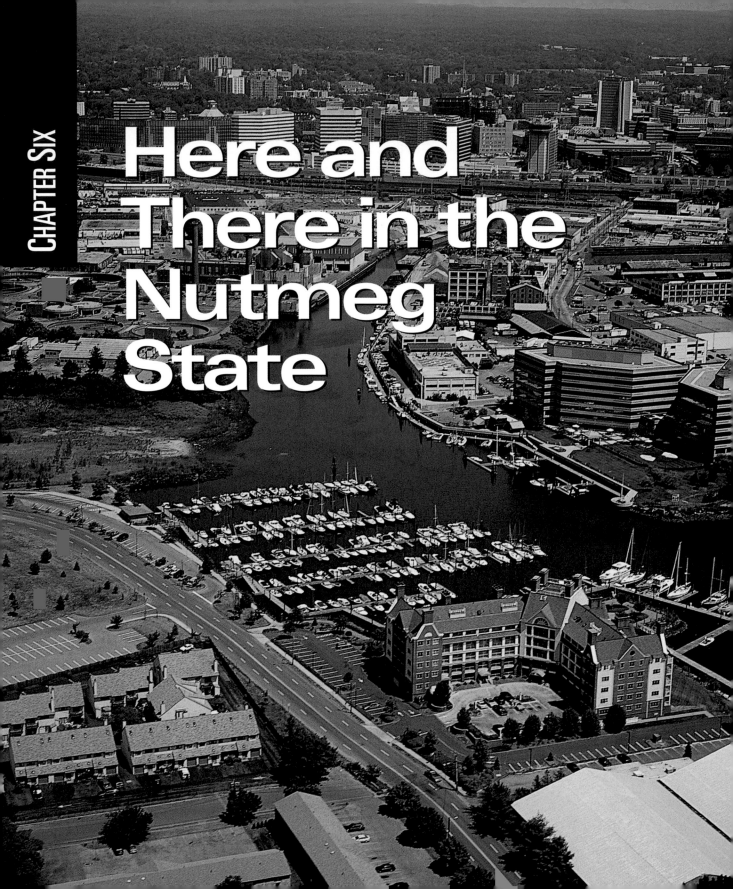

CHAPTER SIX

Here and There in the Nutmeg State

Grazing horses are a common sight in rural Connecticut.

It's less than a day's drive from the sophisticated suburban cities of southwestern Connecticut to the state's quiet, rural northeastern corner. But in a sense, the two regions are worlds apart.

The shoreline from the New York border near Greenwich to just east of New Haven is often called the Gold Coast. It seems more related to New York than to the rest of New England. Skyscrapers house some of the nation's leading corporations in Greenwich and Stamford. Wealthy businesspeople live on large estates near the shore. Each morning, commuter trains rush thousands of briefcase-carrying men and women to New York City's Wall Street and Madison Avenue.

Opposite: Stamford's shoreline

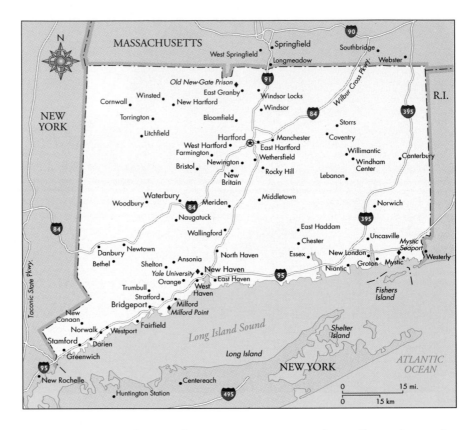

In contrast, the northeastern corner consists of scenic roads, pastures where horses and cows graze, fruit-bearing orchards, and historic villages that still have a pre-Revolutionary aura.

The Gold Coast

Connecticut's Gold Coast is not all high-rises and business. The residents have paid attention to preserving the natural wonders of this lovely corner of New England. On calm summer days, sailboats skim the saltwaters offshore. Those who don't have boats of their own can rent fishing boats or harbor cruise boats at the marinas.

Nature centers in Greenwich, New Canaan, and Westport are open to visitors, and the oldest Audubon center in America is in Fairfield. Natural woodlands, wetlands, and cultivated gardens celebrate nature at the Bartlett Arboretum in Stamford. At the Champion Greenhouse, also in Stamford, the emphasis is on trees and the forest environment.

Exhibits in five buildings of the Historical Society in New Canaan tell the history of the region. Norwalk has had a facelift in recent years. Galleries and arts and crafts shops now occupy renovated stores and factory buildings. The Maritime Aquarium, housed in an old iron factory in Norwalk, explores the marine life

The Maritime Aquarium in Norwalk

The Greatest Showman on Earth

A little boy from Bethel, Connecticut, grew up to be one of the most famous people in the world. P. T. Barnum, as he is usually called, made a fortune—much of it by fooling the public.

Connecticut was a very prim and proper place to live when young Phineas Taylor Barnum was growing up in the early 1800s. There weren't many ways to have fun in those days. Museums and lecture halls were acceptable, but no respectable person would be seen in a theater. However, practical jokes were popular, and P. T. learned a lot about those from his grandfather. One of his early money-making ventures was, in a way, a practical joke.

A newspaper carried a story about a black slave woman who claimed to be 161 years old (this was in 1835). She said she had been President George Washington's nurse when he was an infant. Barnum bought the woman for $1,000, rented a large room, and sold tickets to the public for the privilege of seeing her. Of course both her age and background were fictitious but, as Barnum said, "The American people like to be humbugged."

This was P. T. Barnum's start as an impresario—a person who produces entertainment features. He amused audiences in many different ways. He owned a museum that collected all kinds of unusual items for exhibit. He had a menagerie of exotic animals. And finally, he was part-owner of a circus that uses his name to this day.

As well as Joice Heth, the slave

and maritime heritage of Long Island Sound through hands-on exhibits, boat-building demonstrations, and IMAX film programs.

Bridgeport, once the busiest city in the state, is quieter and less prosperous today. Its many green spaces gave Bridgeport the nickname Park City. A number of these parks were given to the city by its most flamboyant resident, impresario P. T. Barnum.

woman, Barnum took many different kinds of people on the road to entertain the public. The most famous of these was a midget. Barnum named him General Tom Thumb and he became popular and famous around the world. He and Barnum were invited to meet Queen Victoria, and later, President Abraham Lincoln. But Barnum wanted to be known as a patron of the arts, not just a promoter of curiosities. He backed a highly successful concert tour for opera star Jenny Lind, known as the Swedish Nightingale.

Barnum's success was largely due to two outstanding talents. He had an amazing instinct for knowing what would entertain the public, and he was a genius in using the press, both for advertising and for free publicity.

Later in life, Barnum lost his fortune in bad investments. Fires destroyed both his palatial home and his museum. But he bounced back. Interested in politics, he served several terms in the state legislature. A reformer, he supported the abolition of slavery and opposed the powerful railroad lobby. He also served a busy and colorful term as mayor of Bridgeport.

Barnum was past sixty when he got into the circus business. Circuses had existed since ancient times, but Barnum's circus was more elaborate than any seen before. It had more acts, longer parades, larger audiences, and much more flashy publicity. Later he merged his show with another to create the still-famous Barnum and Bailey Circus, "The Greatest Show on Earth." ■

Displays on two floors of the Barnum Museum illustrate the city's impressive manufacturing history. A five-ring miniature circus and mementos of the lives of Barnum and two of his favorite people—the popular General Tom Thumb and opera singer Jenny Lind—are on the museum's third floor. Bridgeport also has a 36-acre (14.5-ha) zoo.

Yale University

Yale College was founded in 1701, making it the third-oldest institution of higher learning in the nation. New Haven became its home in 1716. Elihu Yale, an English merchant, never saw the school that was named for him, but his generous donations to the young struggling college helped it get started. Yale students are nicknamed "Elis."

Several presidents and many other famous people have graduated from Yale. Yale University grants degrees in many professional specialties.

Campus tours led by students are very popular. These tours allow the guests to visit the Beinecke Rare Book and Manuscript Library, the Yale Collection of Musical Instruments, the Peabody Museum of Natural History, and the Yale University Art Gallery, among many landmarks on campus. ■

East of Bridgeport and its suburbs is New Haven, home of the settlers from Massachusetts who founded the New Haven Colony. At one time it was the part-time home of the state capital. Until 1875, the state government regularly moved back and forth between Hartford and New Haven.

Eli Whitney, inventor of the history-changing cotton gin, lived and worked in this town. He also worked on making muskets with interchangeable parts. New Haven has a long and interesting history, but its identity is primarily entwined with its major educational institution—Yale University. New Haven also claims to be the home of the first hamburger and the first pizza sold in the United States.

Children enjoy taking rides on old-fashioned classic vehicles at the Trolley Museum in East Haven. And they can play all kinds of games at a place called The Only Game in Town, in North Haven.

Up the Housatonic River from the Gold Coast is Danbury, once known as Hat City. The Stetson, or "10-gallon hat," was first made here. At one time, about forty factories in the city were turning out hats. A popular attraction in town is the Railway Museum. Classic locomotives and cars stand in a rail yard outside a restored station built in 1902.

Lower Connecticut Valley

Native Americans called these lands *Quinnehtukqut*, meaning "beside the long tidal river" or "long river place." The lower Connecticut River is shallow and filled with sandbars. There's no deep harbor at the mouth of the Connecticut. Because of this, the region was not attractive to industry as other areas to the east and west were. The river,

**The Valley Railroad
Steam Train**

**Opposite: Gillette
Castle**

more than the shore, defines its history. In 1614 a Dutch explorer, Adriaen Block, was the first to note the river on a map.

The scenery, good restaurants, and pretty towns along the lower valley attract visitors from other parts of the state. Old Saybrook, at the river's mouth, was the first home of Yale College. Upriver, in Essex, is the Connecticut River Museum. Housed in an old dock house, it holds paintings, photographs, and exhibits related to the history of the area. Elegant houses in Essex date from the eighteenth and nineteenth centuries. A 1920s steam train carries passengers on a 12-mile (19-km) scenic ride between Essex and Chester. Those who wish to can transfer from the train to a riverboat for a one-hour cruise.

Chester is largely an artists' colony. A plaque on a restaurant wall in Chester pokes fun at the reverence for history so obvious in much of New England. It reads: ON THIS SPOT FEB. 29, 1778, ABSOLUTELY NOTHING HAPPENED.

Three very popular tourist attractions in East Haddam are the Nathan Hale Schoolhouse, where America's first martyr once taught, the Goodspeed Opera House, and Gillette Castle. The American Musical Theatre performs in the 1876 Opera House from May to December each year. Surrounded by a state park, Gillette Castle is an unusual 24-room house with great views of the river. The house was designed a century ago by William

Gillette, a popular stage actor and one of Mark Twain's many friends.

Of Ships and Submarines

Seafaring and ocean life are the center of attention in the southeast corner of Connecticut. Young people can learn a lot about tall ships, sailing, and the sea at Mystic Seaport—a large, famous outdoor museum. Families visit for a day or two; older children can enroll in the varied educational programs. Nearby is the Mystic Marinelife Aquarium, home of more than 6,000 sea creatures. The penguin exhibit is especially fun to see.

New London is the home of the U.S. Coast Guard Academy, one of America's four military academies. Visitors can see a multimedia show about cadet life, tour the museum, and visit the tall ship *Eagle* when it is in port.

Underwater craft are the focus in Groton, home of the U.S. Submarine Force. The world's first nuclear submarine, the USS *Nautilus,* is open to the public.

A few years ago the small Mashantucket Pequot Reservation, a few miles north of Mystic, was off the beaten path. Outsiders knew very little about it. Today, it is one of the most visited spots in the state of Connecticut. The Foxwoods Resort Casino is one of the largest entertainment complexes in the world. Nearby, the 11,000-year history of the Pequot people and their ancestors is interpreted in the impressive new Mashantucket Pequot Museum and Research Center. Visitors descend on an escalator into a re-creation of the Ice Age, where they see glacial formations and a giant mastodon as they may have appeared 18,000 years ago. Then they visit a sixteenth-century village of Woodland Indians, watch a film about the Pequot War, and experiment with interactive computerized exhibits. Another large casino and recreation complex run by Native Americans is the Mohegan Sun, in Uncasville.

The Litchfield Hills

A map of northwestern Connecticut is dotted with green patches that identify state parks and forests, plus blue spots to mark lakes and ponds. Dairy farms occupy some of the spaces in between.

Schoolchildren visit the Mashantucket Pequot Museum

Five nature centers offer interpretive walks and displays. This is the most scenic part of the state and the least densely populated. The state's highest hills are here, an extension of the Massachusetts Berkshires. Hikers are fond of the Appalachian Trail, which is marked and maintained along ridges all the way from Maine to Georgia. Part of it cuts through this lovely corner of Connecticut.

U.S. Highway 7 is a beautiful drive along the Housatonic River. Rocky bluffs stand in majestic contrast to the blazing colors of trees in autumn months. Two picturesque covered bridges span the river. Skiers come to this part of the state, to Woodbury and to Mohawk Mountain Ski Area near Cornwall.

A cannon in Litchfield

The towns of Litchfield, Torrington, and Winsted were early industrial centers. Litchfield manufactured supplies for the Revolutionary army, while brass and copper factories flourished in the other two towns. The industrial days of these historic villages are past. Today, the area is an ideal place for rest and relaxation. Many prominent people who want to escape the hustle and bustle of everyday life have second homes in the Litchfield vicinity. The region has become a refuge for celebrities. Year-round outdoor recreation is the main attraction for visitors, but a few historic landmarks should be mentioned. The Tapping Reeve Law School, in Litchfield, is on the National Register of Historic Places. Built before 1736, the Curtis House, in Woodbury, is Connecticut's oldest inn.

The American Clock and Watch Museum in Bristol honors timepieces, one of the first manufactured products that made Connecticut famous. More than 3,000 clocks and watches are on display. Also in Bristol is a collection of antique carousels and one of the nation's oldest amusement parks—Lake Compounce Theme Park.

Hartford and Surroundings

Hartford, on the Connecticut River, is the state's capital, but government is only one of its activities. People who have shaped its history—and America's—include pioneers in invention and manufacturing, finance and insurance, the arts and education. Its historic landmarks include the nation's oldest statehouse, the oldest free art museum in the country, and the homes of nineteenth-century writers Mark Twain and Harriet Beecher Stowe. Noah Webster's birthplace is in West Hartford.

Hartford's riverfront has been beautified in recent years with picnic areas, playgrounds, and paths for walkers and bikers. Special events are staged in an amphitheater, and excursion boats take visitors out on the river.

Bradley International Airport is north of Hartford, at Windsor Locks. New England Air Museum, at the airport, has more than 80 aircraft on display, some of them dating from 1909. There are gliders, fighters, helicopters, and more. At the nearby Connecticut Trolley Museum, visitors can ride on antique trolley cars.

Colonists mined copper in this region in the early 1700s.

The home of Mark Twain in Hartford

Later, the Old New-Gate Copper Mine in East Granby was used as a prison.

Dinosaurs roamed this valley some 200 million years ago. Their tracks have been preserved in Dinosaur State Park, at Rocky Hill. Visitors can make their own plaster casts of the tracks to take home as souvenirs.

The Quiet Corner

Country roads in northeastern Connecticut wander past orchards, meadows, and vineyards. At one time, manufacturing was as important in northeastern Connecticut as it was in the rest of the state. Textile mills spun out countless yards of cotton and silk thread and tons of cloth bolts. The rural landscape no longer shows much evidence of those days, but the Windham Textile and History Museum in Willimantic tells the story.

The quiet scenery masks a busy history of colonial days too. Farmers from this corner of Connecticut Colony were responsible for persuading the more conservative Puritans living south and west of them to join the Revolution. Revolutionary heroes Israel Putnam and Nathan Hale came from this area, as did Governor Jonathan Trumbull Sr. The Nathan Hale Homestead, in Coventry, is open to the public. Trumbull's, in Lebanon, is one of many landmarks in eastern states that can boast "George Washington slept here."

Several decades after the Revolution, a young woman named Prudence Crandall tried to start a kind of revolution of her own. She had a school for young women in Canterbury, and she decided she would teach black girls along with the others. This was thirty

years before the Civil War. Parents of the white children and other neighbors were horrified. They stoned her house and forced her to close the school. Recently, Miss Crandall has been officially named Connecticut's state heroine. Her home is a museum of African-American, women's, and local history.

A vineyard in rural Connecticut

The Mysterious Frog Fight of Windham Center

It happened more than 200 years ago. Nothing like it ever occurred before or since, as far as anyone knows. Just after midnight on a dark, warm, summer night, a raucous, frightening noise awakened everyone in the neighborhood. Some people thought it was Judgment Day and they fell on their knees in terrified prayer. Others loaded their guns, believing the din was a Native American attack. Still others were sure it was some kind of supernatural event.

When daylight came, one person called the others to come and see a strange and awful sight. He had discovered hundreds of dead bullfrogs all around a small millpond! It seems the pond where the creatures had lived had nearly dried up during a long drought, and the frogs, in desperation, had battled with one another.

Songs, poems, and even an operetta were written about the incident during the next few years. All of them poked fun at the people of Windham Center who had been so terrorized by the noise of fighting frogs. ■

Prudence Crandall's house

The population of the little village of Storrs increases by more than 300 percent when the University of Connecticut is in session. The Connecticut State Museum of Natural History is one of several fine museums on campus. One has a collection of more than 2,000 puppets.

CHAPTER SEVEN

Governing the State

The Cannibals are landing

The American Revolution did not bring about instant democracy in the young nation it created. In Connecticut, political rule was still firmly in the hands of the Puritan aristocrats. Many of the merchants who had opposed separation from England at first actually prospered from their part in supplying and supporting the war. On the other hand, small farmers in the northeastern and northwestern sections of the state were left in bad shape. They had succeeded in persuading Connecticut to join the Revolution, but now they were opposed to the idea of a strong central government.

Two political parties arose from this division. The merchants and their friends were Federalists and Congregationalists. The

A cartoon depicting Washington driving a federal chariot while trying to stop French "cannibals." Jefferson, at far right, tries to stop the wheels of government.

Opposite: The state capitol in Hartford

State Flag and Seal

The Connecticut flag, adopted in 1897, is five feet six inches by four feet four inches (1.6 by 1.3 m), made of azure blue silk, containing the state seal in white silk with the design in natural colors and the border of the seal embroidered in gold and silver. Below the seal is a white streamer, cleft at each end, bordered in gold and brown, bearing in dark blue the motto *Qui Transtulit Sustinet.* The motto means "He who transplanted still sustains." ■

Connecticut's State Symbols

The following official state emblems and symbols have been adopted, by statute, by the Connecticut General Assembly:

State flower: Mountain laurel The General Assembly adopted this as the official state flower. One of the loveliest of native American shrubs, it blooms profusely in Connecticut in late June.

State bird: American robin Actually a thrush, the American robin was named official state bird of Connecticut in 1943. It has a reddish-brown breast and a loud, cheerful song. It is seen throughout North America from Alaska to Virginia in summer. Many robins spend all winter in New England, roosting in evergreens in swampy areas and eating winter berries.

State mineral: Garnet This has been Connecticut's official state mineral since 1977. It is a deep violet-red, very hard stone. Prized as a beautiful gem for jewelry, it has also been important in Connecticut industrially. Its hardness makes it useful as an abrasive, for grinding wheels, saws, and high-quality sanding paper.

State insect: European mantis It is popularly known as a "praying mantis," because it habitually stands on its hind legs with forelegs in a position that makes it look as if it is praying. The mantis is not native to Connecticut, but it can be found throughout the state. Farmers regard it as a friend because it eats aphids, flies, grasshoppers, small caterpillars, and moths.

State ship: USS *Nautilus* Built in Connecticut, this was the world's first nuclear-pow-

church was supported by taxes paid by everyone, even if they belonged to other denominations. The farmers and others opposed to the power of the church supported the Jeffersonian Republican Party.

When the United States became engaged in the War of 1812, the Federalists called it "Mr. Madison's War." They refused to

ered submarine. Named Connecticut's state ship in 1983, it is designated a National Historic Landmark and is permanently berthed next to the Submarine Force Library and Museum at Goss Cove in Groton.

State animal: Sperm whale This was chosen in 1975 as the state animal because of the importance of the whaling industry in Connecticut history and the species' present danger of extinction. The sperm whale has the largest brain of any creature ever known on earth.

State shellfish: Eastern oyster Common in Connecticut's coastal waters, the Eastern oyster was voted the state's shellfish in 1989.

State tree: White oak This commemorates the historic Charter Oak of Hartford.

State folk dance: Square dance This American folk dance was chosen in 1995 by the General Assembly.

State hero: Nathan Hale Remembered for his heroism during the American Revolution, Hale is Connecticut's state hero.

State heroine: Prudence Crandall The woman who tried to give young black girls an education but was forced to close her school is the state heroine.

State composer: Charles Ives The General Assembly chose him as the official state composer in 1991. He lived from 1874–1954. ■

State Song

"Yankee Doodle"

The author of the song's melody is unknown. During the Revolutionary War, however, British surgeon Richard Shackburg composed lyrics that made fun of American troops. In one of the war's battles, colonial militiamen chased British troops while singing the song and making fun of them.

Yankee Doodle went to town,
Riding on a pony,
Stuck a feather in his hat
And called it macaroni.

Yankee Doodle keep it up,
Yankee Doodle dandy,
Mind the music and the step,
And with the folks be handy. ■

Connecticut's Governors

Name	Party	Term	Name	Party	Term
Jonathan Trumbull	None	1776–1784	Joseph Trumbull	Whig	1849–1850
Matthew Griswold	Fed.	1784–1786	Thomas H. Seymour	Dem.	1850–1853
Samuel Huntington	Fed.	1786–1796	Charles H. Pond	Dem.	1853–1854
Oliver Wolcott	Fed.	1796–1797	Henry Dutton	Whig	1854–1855
Jonathan Trumbull II	Fed.	1797–1809	William T. Minor	American†	1855-1857
John Treadwell	Fed.	1809–1811	Alexander H. Holley	Am. and Rep.‡	1857–1858
Roger Griswold	Fed.	1811–1812			
John Cotton Smith	Fed.	1812–1817	William A. Buckingham	Rep.	1858–1866
Oliver Wolcott Jr.	Jeff.-Rep.	1817–1827	Joseph R. Hawley	Rep.	1866–1867
Gideon Tomlinson	Jeff.-Rep.	1827–1831	James E. English	Dem.	1867–1869
John S. Peters	Nat. Rep.	1831–1833	Marshall Jewell	Rep.	1869–1870
Henry W. Edwards	Dem.	1833–1834	James E. English	Dem.	1870–1871
Samuel A. Foot	Whig	1834–1835	Marshall Jewell	Rep.	1871–1873
Henry W. Edwards	Dem.	1835-1838	Charles R. Ingersoll	Dem.	1873–1877
William W. Ellsworth	Whig	1838–1842	Richard D. Hubbard	Dem.	1877–1879
Chauncey F. Cleveland	Dem.	1842–1844			
Roger S. Baldwin	Whig	1844–1846			
Isaac Toucey	Dem.	1846–1847	† Sometimes called Know-Nothing		
Clark Bissell	Whig	1847–1849	‡ Sometimes called Know-Nothing Republican		

back the conflict even after British ships attacked their own shores. The Republicans called the Federalists "unpatriotic."

Oliver Wolcott Jr. was the first Republican to be elected governor of Connecticut, in 1817. Great changes followed.

The Constitutions of 1818 and 1965

A convention met after the election of Oliver Wolcott Jr. to write a new state constitution. One of the most important provisions was the separation of church and state in Connecticut. In addition, the powers

Name	Party	Term	Name	Party	Term
Charles B. Andrews	Rep.	1879–1881	Charles A. Templeton	Rep.	1923–1925
Hobart B. Bigelow	Rep.	1881–1883	Hiram Bingham	Rep.	1925
Thomas M. Waller	Dem.	1883–1885	John H. Trumbull	Rep.	1925–1931
Henry B. Harrison	Rep.	1885–1887	Wilbur L. Cross	Dem.	1931–1939
Phineas C. Lounsbury	Rep.	1887–1889	Raymond E. Baldwin	Rep.	1939–1941
Morgan G. Bulkeley	Rep.	1889–1893	Robert A. Hurley	Dem.	1941–1943
Luzon B. Morris	Dem.	1893–1895	Raymond E. Baldwin	Rep.	1943–1946
O. Vincent Coffin	Rep.	1895–1897	Wilbert Snow	Dem.	1946–1947
Lorrin A. Cooke	Rep.	1897–1899	James L. McConaughy	Rep.	1947–1948
George E. Lounsbury	Rep.	1899–1901	James C. Shannon	Rep.	1948–1949
George P. McLean	Rep.	1901–1903	Chester Bowles	Dem.	1949–1951
Abiram Chamberlain	Rep.	1903–1905	John Lodge	Rep.	1951–1955
Henry Roberts	Rep.	1905–1907	Abraham A. Ribicoff	Dem.	1955–1961
Rollin S. Woodruff	Rep.	1907–1909	John N. Dempsey	Dem.	1961–1971
George L. Lilley	Rep.	1909	Thomas J. Meskill	Rep.	1971–1975
Frank B. Weeks	Rep.	1909–1911	Ella T. Grasso	Dem.	1975–1980
Simeon E. Baldwin	Dem.	1911–1915	William A. O'Neill	Dem.	1980–1991
Marcus H. Holcomb	Rep.	1915–1921	Lowell P. Weicker Jr.	Ind.	1991–1995
Everett J. Lake	Rep.	1921–1923	John G. Rowland	Rep.	1995–

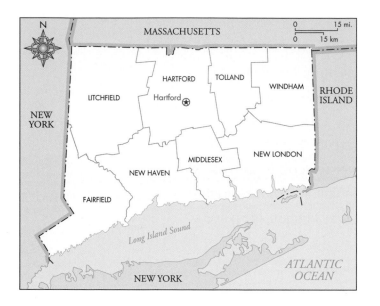

Connecticut's counties

of the three branches of state government—executive, legislative, and judicial—were spelled out. Requirements for voting became less rigid, and provision was made for annual elections and legislative sessions.

Connecticut had governed itself under the Fundamental Orders from 1639 to 1662, when the colony received a Royal Charter. The constitution of 1818 was the foundation of the new state's government until 1965. A serious flaw became evident as the Industrial Revolution led to the growth of cities. The makeup of the legislature was no longer a fair representation of the state's population. Each small town had the same number of representatives as the large cities did. The constitution of 1965 provides for equal representation based on population. It also calls for new district maps to be drawn after each census.

Branches of Government

The 1965 constitution continues the three branches of government. In the executive branch, the governor, lieutenant governor, attorney general, comptroller, secretary of state, and treasurer are all elected by the voters for four-year terms. They can be reelected any number of times.

The General Assembly, or legislative branch, is made up of a 36-member Senate and a 151-member House of Representatives. They are elected for two-year terms. The legislature meets every year.

Connecticut's courts, the judicial branch of state government, consist of a supreme court, an appellate court, and a superior court. The governor appoints judges to these courts and the legislature approves the appointments for eight-year terms. The voters elect judges to the lower (probate) courts for four-year terms.

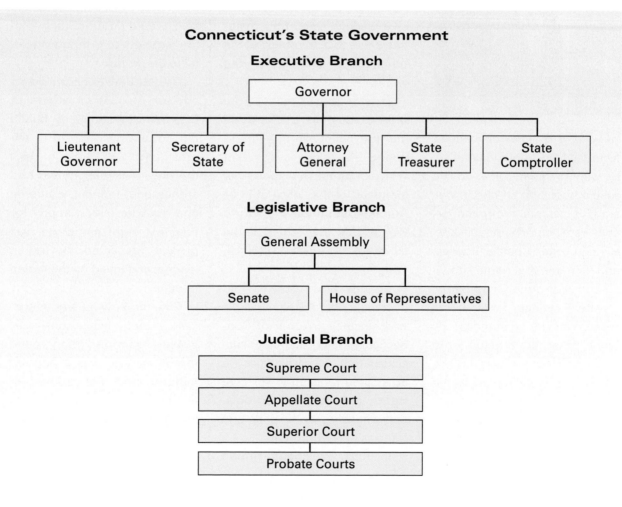

Connecticut's State Government

Executive Branch

Governor

| Lieutenant Governor | Secretary of State | Attorney General | State Treasurer | State Comptroller |

Legislative Branch

General Assembly

| Senate | House of Representatives |

Judicial Branch

Supreme Court

Appellate Court

Superior Court

Probate Courts

Chester Bowles, 1901–1986

He was a Yankee, descended from old New England families. He went to Choate, an exclusive prep school, and to Yale University. His parents and grandparents were staunch Republicans. His name was Chester Bowles, and he made that name known far and wide during his lifetime.

After college, where his record was not outstanding, he went into advertising and achieved great success. In fact, he was a multimillionaire by the age of forty. He had an innovative mind and used new marketing and market research techniques. He is credited with inventing the soap opera as a way to make his clients' products known.

In spite of his business success, Bowles realized he had slid through college without learning much. He decided to give himself a good education. He started a program of intensive reading. One of his major goals was to learn about all the other major countries of the world.

Chester Bowles retired from business in 1941 and devoted the next twenty-eight years to public service. President Franklin Roosevelt appointed him head of the Office of Price Administration during World War II and later, chief of the Office of Economic Stabilization.

By this time, Bowles had become a liberal Democrat. He was elected governor of Connecticut in 1949, after an unsuccessful try two years earlier. He advocated legislation for civil rights, desegregated schools, better housing for the poor, and reforms in government.

In 1951, President Truman appointed Bowles to be the U. S. ambassador to India. Back home again, he was elected to Congress in 1958. Believing the Cold War was dangerous, he advocated better relations with Russia and China. He supported U.S. aid to developing nations. Economic development, he said, would do more than military strength to promote stability in the world.

Chester Bowles became chief advisor on foreign affairs to President John Kennedy, but he did not always agree with the president's decisions. In 1963, the president reappointed him ambassador to India, where he and his wife lived happily for the next eight years. He was greatly respected by Indian leaders and loved by the Indian people.

Chester Bowles was a success in many fields—business, public administration, and diplomacy. He was a popular lecturer and the author of eleven books. In addition, he was a mentor for many younger people who went on to distinguished careers of their own. ■

Local Government

Connecticut has 169 towns, which are small political and land units, comprised of rural and nonincorporated urban areas. Most towns are governed by an elected board of selectmen. The annual town meeting, an old tradition still followed in many small towns in Connecticut and other New England states, is a direct form of democratic government. Voters get together and elect local officials, approve budgets, and vote on other issues. Every voter has a chance to speak his or her mind.

Connecticut has eleven boroughs and twenty cities that are independent of town government. These are heavily populated communities within the towns. Cities have state charters, which they can amend when they wish to. Counties in Connecticut have no governmental jurisdiction.

CHAPTER EIGHT

Earning
a Living

Finance industries have grown in recent years.

Early in Connecticut's history it was easy to see that farming was a difficult way to make a living. Most of the land was too hilly or rocky. But the people were resourceful, and they were good salesmen. Before long, agriculture was largely replaced by manufacturing. Good products were made—things other people wanted to buy. Connecticut peddlers sold them.

Today, one of the state's most important assets is its location. Connecticut is very small, but it is surrounded by customers—people and businesses who want to buy its products. One-third of the U.S. markets and two-thirds of Canada's are within a one-day drive of the state of Connecticut.

Above all else, manufacturing and trade made Connecticut wealthy. In recent years, the state's economy has become more diversified. Finance firms, such as insurance and banking, and service industries are as important as manufacturing and trade. Together, these four sectors produce about 80 percent of the gross state product and employ about 80 percent of Connecticut's workers.

Opposite: A pharmaceutical plant in Groton

Many of America's largest corporations are based in Connecticut. The cities of the southwestern part of the state are almost an extension of New York City, in terms of business. But they are less crowded, less polluted, and have more grass and trees than downtown Manhattan.

Although there are pockets of poverty in the state, the average annual paycheck is the highest in the nation. Also, Connecticut claims first place in the education level of its citizens. That is, it has the highest percentage of people with college degrees. It also has the highest percentage of children aged three to six in school.

Connecticut students in computer class

After many years of prosperity, unemployment rose rather sharply in the state starting in the 1960s. This began to turn around in the mid-nineties. Other indicators were encouraging too. For example, automobile registrations were up, and the construction industry was improving as the number of new housing starts increased.

Manufacturing

Connecticut's leadership in manufacturing owes a great debt to early metalworkers.

These workers developed the machine-tool industry. Machine tools create other tools, and can even re-create themselves. Accurate machine tools make it possible to make accurate and interchangeable parts for other machines. Interchangeable parts,

Sand and gravel are important Connecticut commodities

What Connecticut Grows, Manufactures, and Mines

Agriculture	Manufacturing	Mining
Greenhouse and nursery products	Transportation equipment	Crushed stone
Milk	Machinery	Sand
Eggs	Fabricated metal products	
	Scientific instruments	
	Chemicals	
	Printed materials	
	Electrical equipment	
	Food products	

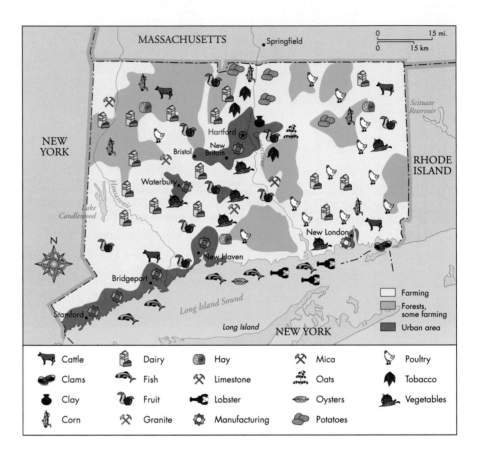

MASSACHUSETTS · Springfield

0 — 15 mi.
0 — 15 km

*Scituate
Reservoir*

NEW
YORK

Hartford

Bristol · New
Britain

RHODE
ISLAND

Waterbury

Housatonic

*Lake
Candlewood*

N

New London

New Haven

Bridgeport ·

Long Island Sound

Stamford ·

Long Island   NEW YORK

☐ Farming
▨ Forests,
some farming
▨ Urban area

	Cattle		Dairy		Hay		Mica		Poultry
	Clams		Fish		Limestone		Oats		Tobacco
	Clay		Fruit		Lobster		Oysters		Vegetables
	Corn		Granite		Manufacturing		Potatoes		

in turn, make mass production possible. Hartford was an early
center of machine-tool manufacture. Mass production also made
it possible to manufacture thousands of sewing machines, and
was directly responsible for the development of the weapons
industry.

Manufacturing was the driving force in the Connecticut economy until about 1960. At that time, half the jobs in the state
were in manufacturing. Then, for various reasons, the number of
people employed in factories started to drop. By the mid-1990s,

Do-It-at-Home Pizza

New Haven people pride themselves on their pizza—also known as tomato pies. Every restaurant has its own secret recipe, and style of baking (coal-fired oven, or brick-oven).

Ingredients:

   3 cups flour

1/2 cup cornmeal

   1 package active dry yeast

1/2 tablespoon sugar

   1 cup water

   1 teaspoon salt

   2 tablespoons olive oil

Ready-made chunky-style pizza sauce to taste

Grated Mozzarella cheese to taste

Toppings of your choice (for a real New Haven flavor, try clams!)

Directions:

In a food processor, blend together flour, cornmeal, yeast, sugar, and salt. While the processor is still running, slowly add the water. Continue to process until the mixture springs away from the sides of the bowl. Process for an additional 20 seconds to knead the dough. If it is too sticky or moist, you may have to add more flour and process for an additional 30–60 seconds. The dough should be warm, smooth, and slightly sticky.

Remove the dough from the food processor and work it into a ball with your hands. Oil a large mixing bowl and place the dough inside. Cover with a damp towel and allow the dough to rise until it has doubled in size, for about 30 minutes to an hour.

Preheat oven to 375° F (191°C). Punch the dough down as much as possible with your hands. Divide it in half and fit each half into a 12-inch (30-cm) pizza pan. If you don't want to use all the dough, you can freeze some for later.

Spread pizza sauce , cheese, and toppings over the pizza and bake for 20–25 minutes, or until the crust has turned a golden brown and the cheese is bubbly.

only about one-fourth of the state's workers were still in manufacturing.

Products of Connecticut's factories are still a major source of income from exports, however. The principal products sold abroad are transportation equipment, industrial machinery, electronics, chemicals and chemical products, and scientific instruments.

Insurance

The insurance industry is as old as the manufacturing industry in Connecticut, and just as important. Shortly after the Revolution some of the city's business leaders got together and agreed to risk some of their money to back a shipowner. They would help him pay for some of his losses in case of bad luck, in return for a share of the profits from successful voyages. Soon after that, the first fire insurance company was established in Norwich. Other fire and marine insurance companies soon followed.

Today, Hartford is known as America's insurance capital. Hartford Fire Insurance Company, started in 1810, is the state's oldest firm of its kind. Two other giants, Aetna and Travelers, as well as dozens of other fire, life, and multiple-line insurance companies, are headquartered in Hartford.

There are fewer people employed in banks, insurance, and real estate than in manufacturing, trade, or services, but these businesses create nearly one-fourth of the state's gross product. The number of jobs in fire, marine, and casualty insurance was growing in the late 1990s.

Wholesale and Retail Trade

In Connecticut, the business of trading started in colonial days, when the Yankee peddlers went door-to-door with wagonloads of goods. Trade, both wholesale and retail, is still a major part of the state's business. More than one out of five people in Connecticut work in trade.

Aetna, in Hartford, is a major insurance company.

Service Industries

More Connecticut people work in service industries than in any other type of industry. Service industries, such as health care, education, and tourism, contribute a great deal to a comfortable standard of living. When the economy is good, service industries become more important. People have money to spend, so they can afford to find ways to make their lives more interesting and fulfilling.

Education

Connecticut's public schools rank well above the average for either New England or the United States as a whole in several areas. It is fourth among the states in the amount of money spent per pupil. It is close to the top among the states in the number of computers available for students.

Choate Preparatory School

Connecticut teachers are well educated. The state has the highest percentage of teachers with advanced degrees in the country. And the ratio of teachers to students is more than twice the national average.

Yale University is the state's oldest and most famous school for higher education. In addition, the state has more than forty other public and independent colleges. Private preparatory schools in the state attract students from all over the country. Some of the best known are Choate, Hotchkiss, and Miss Porter's.

Government

More than 150,000 people in Connecticut hold local and state government jobs. These range all the way from taking care of sewers and waste disposal to presiding over courts. About half the jobs are in public education. After that come positions in hospitals and public health, police departments, financial administration, and transportation. Other employees work in libraries, departments of parks and recreation, fire protection, and a variety of other public services. Every resident of the state benefits from several government services every day.

Educational Firsts in the United States

Connecticut had the:
First law school, 1773
First school for the deaf, 1817
First industrial school, 1819
First theological seminary, 1834
First music school, 1838
First teachers' institute, 1839
First Ph.D. awards, 1861
First state commissioner of education, 1867

Police officers are some of the thousands of citizens that hold government jobs.

CHAPTER NINE

Who Are the Nutmeggers?

Qui *Transtulit Sustinet* is Connecticut's state motto. It means "He who transplanted still sustains." Except for the Pequot and other Native Americans who were here first, all the early Connecticut settlers were transplanted from Europe. For the first 150 years or so, these settlers were very much alike. Almost all of them were white, Anglo-Saxon, and Protestant. That is what is called a homogeneous population.

After the Revolution, many families were very poor and needed a new start. They transplanted themselves from New England to western New York state, Ohio, and points farther west. They made their mark in these new territories and states, especially in politics. Records show that in the year 1831 one-third of the people in the U.S. Senate and one-fourth of those in the House of Representatives were Connecticut-born.

For more than 150 years, Nutmeggers were primarily of European descent.

Immigration

By the middle of the nineteenth century, the tide turned. Now Connecticut factories found they needed more workers than they could find near home. People from continental Europe and Canada

Opposite: A Native American dancer at a festival

were encouraged to come to Connecticut, where there were jobs. New transplants began to arrive.

A severe famine in Ireland forced many people to leave that country. America looked promising. Irish immigrants arrived at the port of New York, and found it easy to get to jobs in New Haven and Hartford. French-Canadians were attracted by the textile mills in eastern Connecticut. Prosperous times between 1890 and 1914 brought many more Europeans to the state—Germans, Italians, Poles, Greeks.

Today's Connecticut neighborhoods reflect ethnic diversity.

Immigration slowed almost to a standstill during the Great Depression. This continued during World War II, except for young men and women who flocked to Connecticut from other states to work in war plants. After the war, other newcomers—African-Americans from the south and Puerto Ricans—added to the mixture of people. The most recent newcomers to Connecticut have arrived from eastern Europe and Asia—Cambodia, Laos, Vietnam, Thailand, and Korea.

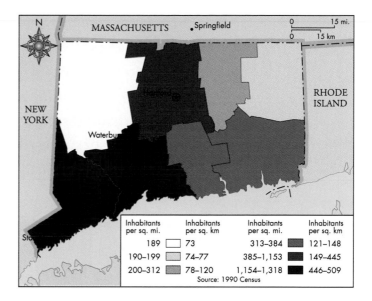

Connecticut's population density

Today about 8 percent of Connecticut's residents are African-Americans, and 10 percent were born in other countries. So most of the state's people are transplants, or descended from transplants. The only exceptions are a few thousand Native Americans, and some of them moved to Connecticut from other parts of the nation. *Qui transtulit sustinet!*

Where They Live

Connecticut has about 3.3 million people. It ranks twenty-seventh in the nation in population. Three-quarters of the people live in the southwest (Gold Coast) and north-central (Hartford) regions. The least populated regions are in the northwest and eastern areas.

The state's largest cities are Bridgeport, Hartford, New Haven, Waterbury, Stamford, Norwalk, New Britain, and Danbury. Although some of the cities seem to run into one another in an

Population of Connecticut's Major Cities (1990)	
Bridgeport	141,686
Hartford	139,739
New Haven	130,474
Waterbury	108,961
Stamford	108,056
Norwalk	78,331

unbroken chain, about one-fifth of the residents of the state still live in rural areas.

Recent cutbacks in manufacturing in Connecticut have resulted in pockets of hardship and poverty in some of the cities. But people who have jobs, especially in high-tech industries, are doing very well. Statistics show that average incomes in Connecticut are among the highest in the nation.

Waterbury is one of the largest cities in Connecticut.

Religion

The Congregational Church, founded by Puritans, was the official state church in Connecticut until 1818 and, as such, it was supported by taxes. This changed when members of other Protestant churches, primarily Episcopalians, Baptists, and Methodists, demanded fair treatment and freedom of worship. By the middle of the 1800s in Connecticut, German Jews and Irish Catholics began to add to the mix of religions. The population of the state was becoming less homogeneous in both origin and religion.

The U.S. Census does not ask questions about religious membership, so exact figures are not available. According to the best estimates, Roman Catholics make up about 40 percent of the total population of the state. Orthodox Christian immigrants from Greece, Russia, Bulgaria, and Romania have also brought their religious practices to Connecticut, especially in Hartford, Waterbury, and Bridgeport. There are a number of Jewish synagogues and Muslim mosques in the state. And the latest newcomers from Asia include Buddhists, Hindus, and followers of other eastern faiths.

CHAPTER TEN

Enjoying Leisure Time

Mountain biking in
Talcott Mountain
State Park

Yes, it's called the land of steady habits, and Connecticut has a no-nonsense tradition of hard work. But few states have more opportunities for enjoying life, whether one is talking about nature's gifts or the creations of men and women. And they're all close together, easily accessible. The state is so small that families can take a day trip from home—no matter where they live—to any other spot in the state and have plenty of time for outdoor activities or sightseeing.

Outdoor Activities

Tucked away from the cities and highways, Connecticut has a lot of wide-open space. Families can relax in fifty-one state parks and nine state forests. Hikers walk the trails and climb the

Opposite: Picking
pumpkins in autumn

mountains. Biking and horseback trails pass through woods, over hills, and across broad green meadows. Campers can find space to pitch their tents or park their trailers in sixty private campgrounds. Bird-watchers and other nature lovers can observe native creatures up close in more than two dozen wildlife preserves, nature sanctuaries, and Audubon centers.

Water is everywhere—rivers, lakes, and the vast Long Island Sound. Swimming, boating, water-skiing, sailing—all these sports are just around the corner from wherever one may be. Fishers can try their luck in both freshwaters and saltwaters. Children enjoy the rides and slides in several water parks. Paddleboats drift lazily on calm lakes; kayaks and canoes shoot the rapids of Connecticut rivers; schooners on the sound take passengers back to yesterday. There are three family amusement parks in Connecticut, and several places to ride on old-fashioned steam trains and trolleys.

Autumn, when the leaves are ablaze with color, is a great time to visit a farm. There are fifteen or more farms in Connecticut where visitors can pet animals and take pony, hay-wagon, carriage, or sleigh rides across the fields. Some farms have orchards where families pick their own apples, or patches for selecting just the right pumpkin to carve into a jack-o-lantern.

Winter changes the landscape, and other sports replace swimming and boating. Bathing suits and snorkeling gear are packed away; skates and skis come out of the closet. As December begins, it's time to visit another farm and find the ideal Christmas tree.

Spectator Sports

Few big-time pro teams have been established in Connecticut, so most Nutmeggers are fans of the major sports teams in New York and Boston. The Hartford Whalers were a National Hockey League team for nearly two decades before moving south to become the Carolina Hurricanes in 1997. For years, the Boston Celtics basketball team played some of their games in Hartford, but the team discontinued this practice in the 1990s. However, Hartford struck back in 1998, when Connecticut governor John Rowland announced a plan to build a new riverside football stadium in downtown Hartford to lure the New England Patriots football team away from Massachusetts. The plan ultimately failed, however.

Minor-league baseball is a favorite spectator pastime in Connecticut every spring and summer. Teams in New Haven, Bridgeport, Norwich, and New Britain regularly draw standing-room-only crowds. By following minor-league teams, fans have the chance to see rising young stars before they hit the big time. On his way to an All-Star career with the Boston Red Sox, Mo Vaughn played minor-league ball in New Britain in the early 1980s. The Norwalk

Opposite: Apple picking is a favorite fall family activity.

Mo Vaughn

native is one of Connecticut's most famous athletes; he now plays for the Anaheim Angels.

Perhaps the most rabidly followed teams in Connecticut are the women's and men's basketball teams of the University of Connecticut. The Lady Huskies were one of the most dominant college teams of the 1990s, making several appearances in the NCAA Final Four. In 1994–1995, UConn legend Rebecca Lobo led the team to an incredible undefeated championship season. On the men's side, UConn won its first national championship in 1999, and it is always among the top-ranked teams in the nation. Coach Jim Calhoun has produced such NBA stars as Cliff Robinson, Ray Allen, and Scott Burrell (who won an NBA championship with the Chicago Bulls in 1998). Late-1990s UConn stars Khalid El-Amin and Richard Hamilton were considered among the best players in college hoops.

College basketball fever is a relatively new phenomenon in Connecticut. A different college tradition dates back to the nineteenth century—the Harvard-Yale football game. Yale University in New Haven and Harvard University in Cambridge, Massachusetts, are both members of the Ivy League—the most prestigious colleges in the nation. Yale and Harvard have maintained a rivalry that goes beyond the classroom and onto the football field. They first faced each other on the gridiron in 1875, and the match eventually became an annual tradition. Today, "The Game" is the most anticipated event of the season, drawing thousands of students and alumni from all over the United States.

Another major sports event in New Haven draws sports fans from around the world every August. The Pilot Pen International

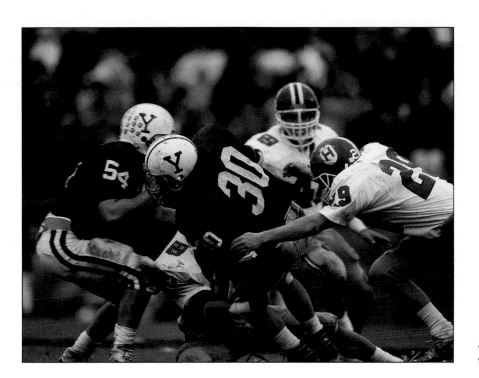

A Harvard–Yale football game

tennis tournament matches up the top players from professional tennis at the Connecticut Tennis Center at Yale University, the third-largest tennis center in the world.

Performing Arts

Summer evenings are filled with the sound of music in many parts of Connecticut. There are chamber-music festivals, jazz festivals, and outdoor concert series. The Hartford Symphony Orchestra presents more than sixty classical and popular concerts each year.

Years ago, when showman P. T. Barnum was growing up, theater was banned in Connecticut as "the work of the devil." Today, theater is a central part of the cultural scene in the state. Faithful fans flock to theaters in several cities.

Dorothy Hamill, Skating Star

She had a dream. It started almost as soon as she put on her first pair of ice skates, when she was eight years old. The skates were hand-me-downs, too big, and almost worn out. But something happened inside the little girl as soon as she could glide on the ice. Skating soon became the most important thing in her life.

Little Dorothy Hamill from Riverside, Connecticut, had a goal—to learn to skate backwards. Before long she learned that as each goal was reached, another took its place: to have skates that really fit well . . . to take skating lessons . . . to win a local competition for juvenile skaters. She won many competitions over the next few years, but she had to accept quite a few losses too. And as she became a better and better skater, her dream, her goal, became the Olympics!

It took many years and thousands of hours of constant practice. Dorothy went to bed early every night and got up before dawn so that she could skate for several hours before going to school. Her parents sacrificed to pay the expenses of training a champion. Dorothy had some of the best skating teachers in the world, custom-made skates, and expensive costumes. She skated in competitions in Canada, Japan, France, Germany, and Czechoslovakia. There was never much time for sightseeing, but she treasured every minute she had.

Dorothy tried hard to make the Olympics skating team in 1972, but failed. Looking ahead to 1976, she captured a U.S. title three years in a row. Then it was Innsbruck, Austria, and fans all over the United States were cheering for Dorothy to "bring home the gold." Her picture was on the cover of *Time* magazine. She put on her mother's rings, for luck, and went on the ice. Moments later, she stood on the winners' podium and listened to the "Star-Spangled Banner." The Olympic gold medal was hers. She had achieved her goal. Her dream had come true.

Other goals soon took the place of this one. Dorothy Hamill went on to win a World Championship in Sweden a few months later. She toured for three years as a star of the Ice Capades skating show. She appeared in several television specials with such Hollywood stars as Gene Kelly, Andy Williams, Perry Como, the Osmonds, and the Carpenters. ■

The Yale School of Drama is nationally known. Its Repertory Theater presents works by budding playwrights. Dramas and musicals are also staged at New Haven's Long Wharf Theatre and the Shubert Performing Arts Center. Goodspeed Opera House in East Haddam is a historic landmark that helps keep the tradition of musical theater alive. The National Theatre of the Deaf, based in Chester, is famous for its innovative work. Summer stock productions and dinner theaters are scattered throughout the state.

The famous U.S. playwright and Nobel prizewinner Eugene O'Neill, spent his childhood summers in Connecticut and used it as the setting for some of his plays. Many actors, as well as other artists, have lived in Connecticut at one time or have second homes there at present. Four well-known actors, all of them Oscar-winners, are residents Katharine Hepburn, Meryl Streep, Paul Newman, and his wife, Joanne Woodward. Hepburn was born into a prominent Hartford family. Meryl Streep is an alumna of the Yale School of Drama. The Newmans live in Connecticut. Newman's Own Inc., the company that produces popcorn, salad dressings, and other food products, is based in Westport and is unique in that it donates all of its profits to charity.

Eugene O'Neill

Museums

The Wadsworth Atheneum, one of the nation's oldest art museum, has a collection of nearly 50,000 objects that cover a 5,000-year history of art. On display there are bronzes from ancient Egypt, Greece, and Rome. Other works cover many periods up to contemporary times. Especially outstanding is a large collection of U. S. paintings of the Hudson River School.

More than a dozen other art museums and collections are scattered throughout Connecticut. Eleven sites have joined together to create the Connecticut Impressionist Art Trail.

Nearly every town in the state has a historical museum or a collection of historical objects in a home dating from colonial or Victorian times. And there is a fascinating variety of special collections, such as the Clock and Watch Museum in Bristol, Tobacco Museum in Windsor, Farm Implement Museum in Bloomfield, Doll and Toy Museum in Coventry—and many others.

Niantic, New Haven, Manchester, and New Britain each has a hands-on children's museum.

The Wadsworth Atheneum

Writers and Readers

Connecticut has not produced as many famous writers as some other states, but it has produced readers. According to state statistics, a higher percentage of people use public library facilities in Connecticut than in any other state. The *Hartford Courant* has been published continuously since 1764—longer than any other newspaper in the country.

Daniel Wadsworth, Philanthropist

Daniel Wadsworth (far right), born in 1771, was Connecticut's first major philanthropist. His was a wealthy family, and he was always interested in helping people less fortunate than himself. He distributed food to people in need. He gave money to help build Hartford Retreat, the state's first mental hospital. He also helped organize the Hartford Orphan Asylum.

But Wadsworth's greatest achievement was the establishment of the first public art museum in America. He gave the land, raised funds to construct the building, and donated paintings to start the collection. Wadsworth was married to Faith Trumbull, daughter of Governor Jonathan Trumbull Jr. and niece of the painter John Trumbull. ■

The Clock and Watch Museum in Bristol

A Master Storyteller

Sam Clemens thought he would spend his life as a riverboat pilot on the Mississippi. In Florida, where he was born in 1835, and in Hannibal, Missouri, where he grew up, Sam spent many hours on the riverbank, watching the boats and barges and skows float by or put in to shore. Tales told by rivermen inspired daydreams of faraway places and exciting adventures.

Sam was only twelve when his father died and he had to go to work. The local newspaper printer took him on as an apprentice. He learned to set type and do a little reporting. Books took the place of school for Sam, and he began to read a great deal. Over the next few years he worked briefly for newspapers in Hannibal and St. Louis in Missouri, as well as papers in New York, Iowa, and Ohio. He finally got the chance to become a riverboat pilot and spent four years sailing down the Mississippi.

But Sam was destined to be a writer; he couldn't escape it. Wherever he went, he found stories to tell. And he couldn't help seeing the funny side of life, in almost everything he wrote. Sometimes this got him into trouble, especially when he poked fun at important people in print.

Sam Clemens began using the pen name of Mark Twain while writing a newspaper column in Nevada. That's the name that brought him fame and fortune. He never took his writing very seriously. He thought of himself as primarily a humor writer, and he didn't think that was very important work. Once he wrote that he had realized, after fifteen years of success, that he had no talent for writing. But by that time he couldn't give it up, he said, "because I was already famous."

The Clemens family settled in Hartford, Connecticut, in 1874. They built a wonderful house on a hill, next door to another author—Harriet Beecher Stowe. Twain began using a new machine, just invented, called a typewriter. His world-famous novel *Tom Sawyer* was the first typed manuscript ever sent to a publisher.

Besides *Tom Sawyer,* some of Twain's most famous books are *Innocents Abroad, Life on the Mississippi, The Prince and the Pauper, The Adventures of Huckleberry Finn,* and *A Connecticut Yankee in King Arthur's Court.*

Mark Twain had financial ups and downs, but his popularity never lessened. He was always in great demand as a public lecturer. His later years were filled with sorrow over the deaths of his wife and two of his daughters. But all over the world people still laugh at his humor and take great delight in reading his books. ■

Two foremost Connecticut authors, Mark Twain and Harriet Beecher Stowe, wrote books that had a tremendous effect on nineteenth-century American society. In their older years, they were next-door neighbors in Hartford. Both were outspoken in their opinions on the important and controversial issues of their day— slavery, women's suffrage, temperance, and the treatment of handicapped and unfortunate people. Stowe made Americans search their consciences on the subject of slavery. Twain made them laugh at their own foolish ways.

Other writers from Connecticut have included the children's writer and illustrator Maurice Sendak, whose *Where The Wild Things Are* is a continual favorite with young and old alike. Writers F. Scott Fitzgerald and Peter DeVries were also active in Connecticut.

America owes much to the people who lived in Connecticut during the past four centuries. They included the wise men who helped shape our nation's system of government and the innovators who invented and produced so many of the products we use every day. We also remember the reformers who worked to help people in need, and the writers and artists whose work continues to give us pleasure.

Timeline

United States History

1607 The first permanent British settlement is established in North America at Jamestown.

1620 Pilgrims found Plymouth Colony, the second permanent British settlement.

1776 America declares its independence from England.

1783 The Treaty of Paris officially ends the Revolutionary War in America.

1787 The U.S. Constitution is written.

1803 The Louisiana Purchase almost doubles the size of the United States.

1812–15 U.S and Britain fight the War of 1812.

1861–65 The North and South fight each other in the American Civil War.

Connecticut State History

1631 Robert Rich and eleven other Englishmen claim title to land that is now Connecticut.

1636 Thomas Hooker leads his party to Hartford. Hartford, along with Wethersfield and Windsor, becomes the Connecticut Colony.

1662 Connecticut Colony receives a royal charter from King Charles II. The charter is revoked fifteen years later.

1784 Tapping Reeve Law School, the first law school in the United States, is established. Connecticut begins to abolish slavery.

1788 Connecticut becomes the fifth state to ratify the Constitution on January 9.

1792 Eli Whitney develops the cotton gin in New Haven.

1818 Connecticut adopts a new state constitution to replace the 1662 charter. Church and state are separated and the power of the governor is expanded.

1839 The *Amistad* is discovered in Long Island Sound.

United States History

The United States is **1917-18** involved in World War I.

The stock market crashes, **1929** plunging the United States into the Great Depression.

The United States fights in **1941-45** World War II.

The United States becomes a **1945** charter member of the United Nations.

The United States fights **1951-53** in the Korean War.

The U.S. Congress enacts a series of **1964** groundbreaking civil rights laws.

The United States **1964-73** engages in the Vietnam War.

The United States and other **1991** nations fight the brief Persian Gulf War against Iraq.

Connecticut State History

1938 The Great Hurricane destroys property and claims many lives in Long Island Sound.

1965 Connecticut's constitution is amended so that members of the state's lower house are elected on the basis of population.

1974 Ella Grasso is elected governor—the first woman to be elected governor of a state instead of succeeding her husband to the office.

1983 The Mashantucket Pequot Indian tribe gains recognition by the federal government, settling a claim to land in Connecticut.

1991 Under Governor Lowell Weicker, Connecticut residents pay income tax for the first time in order to balance the state's budget.

1992 A gambling casino opens on the Mashantucket Pequot reservation.

Fast Facts

The capitol

Robin

Statehood date	January 9, 1788, the 5th state
Origin of state name	From Mohegan and other Algonquin words meaning "long river place" or "beside the long tidal river"
State capital	Hartford
State nicknames	Constitution State, Nutmeg State, Provision State
State motto	*Qui Transtulit Sustinet* (He who transplanted still sustains)
State bird	American robin
State flower	Mountain laurel
State shellfish	Eastern oyster
State animal	Sperm whale
State insect	European mantis
State mineral	Garnet
State song	"Yankee Doodle"
State tree	White oak

Mystic Seaport

Total area; rank	5,544 sq. mi. (14,359 sq km); 48th
Land; rank	4,845 sq. mi. (12,549 sq km); 48th
Water; rank	699 sq. mi. (1,810 sq km); 36th
Inland water; **rank**	161 sq. mi. (417 sq km); 47th
Coastal water; **rank**	538 sq. mi. (1,393 sq km); 11th
Geographic center	Hartford, at East Berlin
Latitude and longitude	Connecticut is located approximately between 41° 00′ and 42° 03′ N and 71° 47′ and 73° 40′ W
Highest point	Mount Frissell, 2,380 feet (725 m)
Lowest point	Sea level, at Long Island Sound
Largest city	Bridgeport
Number of counties	8
Population; rank	3,295,669 (1990 census); 27th
Density	658 persons per sq. mi. (254 per sq km)
Population distribution	79% urban, 21% rural

A Nutmegger

Ethnic distribution (does not equal 100%)	
White	86.99%
African-American	8.34%
Hispanic	6.48%
Asian and Pacific Islanders	1.54%
Native American	0.20%
Other	10.00%

Record high temperature	105°F (41°C) at Waterbury on July 22, 1926

Mountain laurel

Record low temperature	–32°F (–36°C) at Falls Village on February 16, 1943
Average July temperature	71°F (22°C)
Average January temperature	26°F (–3°C)
Average annual precipitation	47 inches (119 cm)

Natural Areas and Historic Sites

National Scenic Trail

Appalachian National Scenic Trail is in the northwest corner of Connecticut

National Historic Site

Weir Farm National Historic Site is named after the American Impressionist J. Alden Weir, who spent summers here. It includes his studio, home, barns, and other buildings.

State Parks

Hammonasset Beach State Park is the largest of the parks that border Long Island Sound

Dinosaur State Park has a giant dome that contains dinosaur tracks from 185 million years ago.

Talcott Mountain State Park's Heublein Tower has a view of four states. It lies in the middle of the Farmington River Valley.

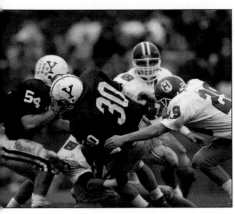

A Harvard–Yale football game

Sports Teams

NCAA Teams (Division 1)
Central Connecticut State Blue Devils
Fairfield University Stags
University of Connecticut Huskies
University of Hartford Hawks
Yale University Bulldogs

Cultural Institutions

Libraries

The Connecticut State Library (Hartford) has several specialized collections, including the History and Genealogy Unit that provides access to historical materials about the state's citizens.

Yale University Library (New Haven) houses the Beinecke Rare Book and Manuscript Library and has extensive collections on African and Judaic cultures.

The University of Connecticut Library system comprises several specialized libraries, such as the Homer Babbidge Library in Storrs and the Archives and Special Collections in the Dodd Research Center.

The Connecticut Historical Society is a library, museum, and education center, and has some of the most distinguished library holdings in New England. It is the seventh oldest historical society in the nation.

The Wadsworth Atheneum

Museums

The Aldrich Museum of Contemporary Art in Ridgefield is an influential venue for cutting-edge paintings and sculpture.

The Lyman Allyn Art Museum in New London has a variety of Connecticut paintings, furniture, and decorative arts from the eighteenth and nineteenth centuries.

The Wadsworth Atheneum in Hartford is one of America's oldest public art museums. It has more than 50,000 pieces of art.

The Peabody Museum of Natural History at Yale University contains a 110-foot (33-m) mural called *The Age of Reptiles* along with dinosaur bones in its Great Hall of Dinosaurs. The museum was founded in 1866.

Performing Arts

Connecticut has two opera companies, two symphony orchestras, two dance companies, and three professional theater companies.

Universities and Colleges

Connecticut had nineteen public and twenty-three private institutions of higher learning in the mid-1990s.

Annual Events

January–March

U.S. Eastern Ski Jumping Championships in Salisbury (February)

April–June

Garlicfest in Fairfield (April)

Dogwood Festival in Fairfield (May)

Lobster Weekend in Mystic (May)

Farmington Antiques Weekend in Farmington (June)

July–September

Greater Hartford Open Golf Tournament in Cromwell (June)

Blessing of the Fleet in Stonington (early July)

Ancient Fife and Drum Corps Muster and Parade in Deep River (July)

Antique and Classic Boat Rendezous (July)

Barnum Festival in Bridgeport (July)

Jazz Festival in New Haven (July)

Riverfest in Hartford and East Hartford (July)

Connecticut Traditional Jazz Festival in Moodus (August)

Mystic Outdoor Arts Festival (August)

Native American Festival in Haddam (August)

Norwalk Oyster Festival (September)

Fall New Haven Antiques Show (September)

October–December

Connecticut Scottish Festival (October)

Christmas Torchlight Parade in Old Saybrook (December)

P. T. Barnum

Famous People

Ethan Allen (1738–1789)	Revolutionary soldier
Phineas Taylor Barnum (1810–1891)	Showman
Catherine Beecher (1800–1878)	Educator
Henry Ward Beecher (1813–1887)	Clergyman
Lyman Beecher (1775–1863)	Clergyman
Chester Bowles (1901–1986)	Public official
John Brown (1800–1859)	Abolitionist

Eugene O'Neill

Samuel Clemens (Mark Twain) (1835–1910)	Writer
Samuel Colt (1814–1862)	Inventor
Prudence Crandall (1803–1890)	Educator, state heroine
Wilbur L. Cross (1862–1948)	Educator, public official
Jonathan Edwards (1703–1758)	Theologian
Thomas Gallaudet (1787–1851)	Educator
William Hooker Gillette (1853–1937)	Actor
Charles Goodyear (1800–1860)	Inventor and manufacturer
Nathan Hale (1755–1776)	Soldier
Katharine Hepburn (1907–)	Actor
Elias Howe (1819–1867)	Inventor
Collis Potter Huntington (1821–1900)	Railroad builder
Edwin Land (1910–1991)	Inventor
John Pierpont Morgan (1837–1913)	Financier
Ralph Nader (1934–)	Reform activist
Paul Newman (1925–)	Actor
Frederick Law Olmsted (1822–1903)	Landscape architect
Eugene O'Neill (1888–1953)	Playwright
Gifford Pinchot (1865–1945)	Forester
Rosa Ponselle (1897–1981)	Singer
Israel Putnam (1718–1790)	Revolutionary War general
Abraham Ribicoff (1910–)	Public official

Noah Webster

Igor Sikorsky (1880–1972)	Inventor
Harriet Beecher Stowe (1811–1896)	Author
John Trumbull (1756–1843)	Painter
Jonathan Trumbull Sr. (1710–1785)	Public official
Noah Webster (1758–1843)	Lexicographer
Eliazer Wheelock (1711–1779)	Clergyman and educator
Eli Whitney (1765–1825)	Inventor
Emma Hart Willard (1787–1870)	Educator

To Find Out More

History

- Fradin, Dennis Brindell. *Connecticut*. Danbury, Conn.: Children's Press, 1997.
- Fradin, Dennis Brindell. *The Connecticut Colony.* Chicago: Childrens Press, 1990.
- Gelman, Amy. *Connecticut*. Minneapolis: Lerner, 1992.
- Thompson, Kathleen. *Connecticut*. Austin, Tex.: Raintree/Steck Vaughn, 1996.
- Wills, Charles A. *A Historical Album of Connecticut*. Brookfield, Conn.: Millbrook Press, 1995.

Fiction

- Avi. *Windcatcher.* New York: Simon & Schuster, 1991.

- Murphy, Jim. *Young Patriot: The American Revolution as Experienced by One Boy.* New York: Clarion Books, 1996.

Biographies

- Bland, Celia. *Harriet Beecher Stowe.* New York: Chelsea House, 1993.
- Collins, David. *Noah Webster: Master of Words.* New York: Fromm International, 1989.
- King, David C. *Benedict Arnold and the American Revolution.* Woodbridge, Conn.: Blackbirch, 1998.
- Wright, David, and Mike White (illustrator). *P. T. Barnum.* Austin, Tex.: Raintree/Steck-Vaughn, 1997.

Websites

- **State of Connecticut**

  http://www.state.ct.us/

  The official website for the state of Connecticut

- **Connecticut Historical Society**

  http://www.chs.org/

  The main web page for the organization

Addresses

- **Governor's Office**

  State Capitol

  210 Capitol Avenue

  Hartford, CT 06106

- **Connecticut State Library**

  231 Capitol Avenue

  Hartford, CT 06106

- **Connecticut Office of Tourism**

  Department of Economic and Community Development

  505 Hudson Street

  Hartford, CT 06106

Index

Page numbers in *italics* indicate illustrations.

Meet the Author

Sylvia McNair was born in Korea and believes she inherited a love of travel from her missionary parents. She grew up in Vermont. After graduating from Oberlin College, she held a variety of jobs, married, had four children, and settled in the Chicago area. She now lives in Evanston, Illinois. She is the author of several travel guides and more than a dozen books for young people published by Children's Press.

"New England is my favorite section of the United States. I've always been interested in its history and love its scenery. I spent a summer working in Connecticut during my college years. I go to see relatives in that state often, usually several times a year. It was a special pleasure to visit the state's landmarks while writing this book. As a child, Harriet Beecher Stowe and Mark Twain were two of my favorite writers, so it was great fun to see their homes in

Hartford. I enjoyed Mystic Seaport because it brings alive what life was like during the great seafaring days of early America.

"Writing a book about a specific state or country gives me the chance to learn as much as I can about the subject. I read, interview people, and see what I can find on the Internet. When I'm reading or writing about a particular place, I'm really there, in my imagination. Each state has its own history, its own landscape, its own personality. I hope this book will give young people a desire to learn more about Connecticut and other states."

McNair has traveled in all fifty states and more than forty countries.

Photo Credits

Photographs ©:

AllSport USA: 119, 131 (Damian Strohmeyer), 7 bottom, 120 (USOC)

Archive Photos: 23, 34, 43, 44 right, 134

Art Resource, NY: 26 (National Portrait Gallery, Smithsonian Institution), 33, 37

Brown Brothers: 13, 17, 19, 30 left, 46

Connecticut Historical Society: 20, 32

Corbis-Bettmann: 6 bottom, 48, 50, 51, 74, 96, 121, 133 (UPI), 6 top right, 7 top right, 18, 27, 30 right, 38, 69, 124, 135

Culver Pictures: 15, 22, 44 left, 47

Dave Sigworth: 73

David J. Forbert: back cover, 11, 55, 81, 86, 98

Envision: 103 (Rudy Muller)

Gamma-Liaison, Inc.: 57 (Brian Smith)

John Muldoon: cover, 68, 85, 99, 115

McConnell & McNamara: 2, 8, 35, 63, 67, 76, 82, 105, 106, 116, 123 bottom, 130 (Jack McConnell)

National Geographic Image Collection: 112 (Joel Sartore)

New England Stock Photo: 56 (Leonard Friend), 6 top center, 53, 64, 65, 70, 87, 88, 122, 128 top, 132 (Michael Giannaccio), 78 (William Hubbell), 100, 114 (Brenda James), 107, 110, 129 bottom (Pat Lynch), 7 top left, 71, 108 (Lou Palmieri), 7 top center, 60 (David E. Rowley), 79 (Paul R. Turnbull)

North Wind Picture Archives: 9, 12, 21, 25, 29, 40, 42, 109

Photofest: 41

SportsChrome East/West: 118 (Scott Cunningham)

Stock Montage, Inc.: 28

The New York Historical Society: 89

Visuals Unlimited: 6 top left, 90, 128 bottom (Barbara Gerlach), 101 (Jeff Greenberg), 83 (Science), 91 (Gilbert Twiest), 62 (Tom J. Ulrich), 39, 129 top

Wadsworth Atheneum: 123 top (Gift of Mr. Faneuil Adams)

Maps by XNR Productions, Inc.